WHAT PEOPLE ARE SA\
DELIVER BETTER R

CU00924696

This book is for executives who realize th
than just coders or a project management team, and who are looking
to optimize the way their team works. It offers practical guidance
without providing process recipes, being too philosophical, or treating
employees and contributors as mere "resources."

~ **Tal Reichert**, CTO, Greenscreens.ai

This is a must-read for software development leaders and executives
striving for excellence. Its insights make it a game-changer. Broza's
brilliant emphasis on viewing software organizations as a cohesive
system of value delivery hits the mark, and his 10 powerful strategies
for optimizing value delivery are a treasure trove of actionable wisdom.
As an R&D leader, I found the book's focus on incremental improvement
and practical execution particularly refreshing.

~ **Dinah Davis**, former VP of R&D, Arctic Wolf Networks

Product people like frameworks but hate rules, and favor simplicity to
complexity, but people + tech + orgs tangle up in complicated ways. This
book unravels that knot with simple and clear advice that considers the
whole messy human system, not just one department or specialty.

~ **Andrew McGlinchey**, VP Product, PropertyGuru, ex-Microsoft, ex-Google

Discover a people-first systematic approach in Gil Broza's groundbreaking
book on technology product development and solution delivery. This
book is your compass to achieving remarkable results in this ever-
evolving space, blending strategic insight and practical steps in every
chapter. It will transform the way you approach your role.

~ **TK Balaji**, CIO, Post Consumer Brands

So many leaders attempt to transform their organization by changing
everything, but I've never seen that succeed. With Gil's book, leaders can
now apply specific changes to create a more effective system of work.
That's how to do a transformation of any kind.

~ **Johanna Rothman**, Consultant, author of *Manage Your Project Portfolio*

Clearly and concisely written, this book presents a solid foundation
followed by practical improvement strategies for advancing the
performance of an organization. Particularly inspiring to me is the
treatment of humanity in our professional lives as an asset rather than
trying to minimize it in the name of efficiency.

~ **Christopher Marsh**, former VP Engineering at Comcast

Gil's book provides a compelling guide for today's VUCA leaders looking for practical, systemic, people-first delivery strategies. Chock full of helpful advice, real-world stories, and context-based awareness, I can't think of a better guide for today's organizational leaders.

~ **Bob Galen**, Agile Coach, Agile Moose

Gil clearly understands the execution challenges that organizations face. On more than one occasion it felt like I was not simply reading a chapter in a book but receiving custom advice based on his personal observations. Since finishing the book, I've been more mindful of the overall system and pull from the contents often when meeting with leaders.

~ **Alesha Foy**, Director Enterprise Agility, BECU

This book is an invaluable resource for leaders who seek to foster a positive culture and build strong and effective product development teams.

~ **Alon Sabi**, Head of Engineering, Breadstack Technologies

Why does a great idea or design fail to result in a great product? It takes many different people, with diverse skills, collaborating effectively to create valuable products. This book gives you an actionable plan to break out of the silos that are holding your organization back from achieving its potential.

~ **Jeremy Kriegel**, UX Leader, Host of the Saving UX podcast

If you're looking to take your organization to the next level, this book is quite literally for you. Gil has masterfully created a simple, straightforward approach that will guide you every step of the way while giving you the freedom to adapt it to your unique context.

~ **David Wallace**, Principal Agile Coach, Xero

As a product leader, I find this book to be a refreshing departure from prescriptive approaches, offering instead a valuable set of insightful strategies and questions to guide both leaders and teams in unleashing their full potential. With a useful self-assessment tool as a guide, it's an effective resource for organizations seeking genuine improvement in how they deliver results.

~ **Steve Rogalsky**, VP Product Management

Gil introduces us to a tailored approach for greater business agility. Giving clear, step-by-step guidance and observable metrics, he helps the reader achieve optimum fitness for their organization. People using the Agile Fluency® Model have asked us: How do we achieve organizational fluency? Deliver Better Results has the answer to that question.

~ **Diana Larsen**, Leadership Agility Advisor, author, *Lead Without Blame* and other books

Read this book today; start improving your delivery capabilities tomorrow. Gil Broza offers a simple and pragmatic model—grounded in real-life experiences—for assessing current state and introducing systemic change while keeping people firmly in the foreground. I'm looking forward to bringing this empirical and human-centered approach to the leaders I work with to help them address crucial delivery challenges right away, no matter where they're starting from.

~ **Ellen Grove**, Business Agility Coach, Agile Partnership

Deliver Better Results provides a motivating approach to hone the system you've always wanted at the scale you've always dreamed of!

~ **David Johnson**, Principal Software Engineer & DevOps Facilitator, Skillsoft

This book exemplifies having a "people first" approach. It explains in detail how to enable an entire human system inside a bigger complex context.

~ **Malene Krohn**, VP, Excellence in Product Development, Leadership, and Operations, SimCorp

Deliver Better Results is an essential read for forward-thinking leaders. It provides a transformative roadmap to effective product development and solution implementation by incorporating human-first insights with systems thinking. Regardless of your organization's approach—Agile, hybrid, or traditional—the strategies within these pages empower you to improve your value delivery.

~ **Moe Ali**, CEO, Product Faculty

This book strikes the right balance, giving you the steps to improve your organization while not prescribing a detailed formula that might not apply. Instead, it gives you strategies with examples from various companies and forces you to think about what would work for your specific situation.

~ **Tim Grant**, Sr. Technical Program Manager, Dejero Labs

A valuable leadership guide for exploring the bigger picture of systems and their impacts on delivery.

~ **Tricia Broderick**, Leadership Advisor, Ignite Insight + Innovation

The pragmatic guidance in this awesome book can be applied to any team or organization that wants to learn about their system of work and how to improve their outcomes incrementally.

~ **Debbie Brey**, Enterprise Agile COE Leader, The Boeing Company

Deliver Better Results

How to Unlock Your Organization's Potential

GIL BROZA
FOREWORD BY JEFF GOTHELF

ISBN print: 978-0-9880016-7-1
ISBN ebook: 978-0-9880016-8-8

Cover design: BookCoverExpress.com

Editing: StoriesRulePress.com

The publisher offers discounts on this book when ordered in quantity for bulk purchases or special sales, which may include electronic versions. For more information, please contact:

Gil Broza
(416) 302-8120
gbroza@3PVantage.com

Published by 3P Vantage Media

CONTENTS

FOREWORD

Recently, I found myself working as part of a team with a large, multi-national financial services organization. Our mandate was to level up the skills of their product management practice — move them away from being foremen of a feature factory and toward the navigators of uncertainty they needed to be. We spent the better part of a year delivering training and coaching. We taught the principles of a Lean approach to product management. We promoted the concepts of managing for outcomes and continuous improvement.

The desire for improvement was evident with the team and their leadership. The individual training with the product managers went well. They understood the ideas and demonstrated how they'd put them into action on their specific initiatives. And yet, the larger transformation wasn't happening.

After many months of similar efforts, we decided to try a new approach. We expanded the training and coaching to the entire product development team — not just the product managers. We invited engineers, testers, delivery leads, designers and business stakeholders. We gave them the same training we had given the product managers — the same content, the same delivery. The results were dramatically different.

Their conversations were more robust. Discussions about delivering value to their customers grew from "Here's what you should build:" to "How do we know this is the best approach?" Many of the leaders who took part were shocked to learn that this was the first time some of these folks had ever spoken to each other directly. The end result was a cohesive system, grounded in a shared understanding of their purpose and their desired way of working.

While this change gave the transformation a significant push forward, it was only the beginning of the department's improvement towards delivering better results. They began to see themselves as a whole team, what Gil Broza calls "a system" in this book. Their decisions began to change from local optimizations to global improvements. The new transparency between discipline silos made obvious their inefficiencies while ensuring that everyone, regardless of role, knew how their work was impacting their customers and users.

By treating the entire software delivery organization as a system, it became obvious to us and to the client where there were gaps in its fitness for purpose. When we worked strictly with the product managers, those gaps were local. Working with the entire system, we recognized the improvements that would make much more impactful changes to how well this team built digital products and made their customers more successful.

All too often we try to boil down the challenges in our organization to a single, explicit root cause. "The developers are taking too long," or "The product managers change their mind too often." Then we apply local solutions that don't address the whole system. This insightful and accessible book will help you think and act differently for better results.

Without broadly prescribing popular frameworks, what Gil is sharing in this book is a practical, simple way to view your entire system of work and assess its health. Then, rather than paint a beautiful picture of a perfect future state, the book walks you through a sequential series of strategies and supporting techniques to incrementally make your system of work better. Gil's approach reduces the risk of changing too fast and gives clear go/no-go criteria for applying the next set of strategies. Your company will benefit from these methods and your teams will thank you.

— Jeff Gothelf
Author, *Lean UX* and *Sense & Respond*

INTRODUCTION

When I started my career in software development, the prevailing method of work was project-oriented and plan-driven. Later, other methods appeared, some becoming very popular. Each took a different approach to individuals and teams, to projects and products, and to processes and practices. Yet, each made the same claim: "This is how you'll deliver value successfully."

In reality, however, no company uses just one work method exclusively and exactly as prescribed. Every company's way of conceiving, developing, and delivering products and solutions is a mix of ideas from multiple methods, from management literature, and from its own people's brains. It's never perfect — and sometimes, far from perfect — so leaders try to improve it, whether gradually or via "transformation," with varying levels of success.

In 2021, I started to explore this question: "Even though all companies are different, what do all successful improvements to value delivery have in common?" My objective was to develop a simple model that leaders could use to improve their way of working whether it was product-oriented or project-oriented, plan-driven or agile or hybrid, based on a popular framework or home-grown.

The result of my exploration is a set of ten sequential and incremental strategies to apply across a value delivery system. They produce a real and sustainable increase in its fitness for purpose — meaning that the system better helps the company achieve its mission and objectives — without prescribing what form that must take. I based the model on my experience and observations from 30 years in the world of software development, the last 19 of which I've spent as coach and consultant to over 100 organizations of all sizes and industries. I've iterated over it using feedback from dozens of senior managers and other consultants. Most importantly, I stand on the shoulders of giants too numerous to name here.

And now, I've captured the model in this: the minimum viable book for improving value delivery. Since there's so much to know and do on this front, this book could have easily been 1,000-pages long, and you probably wouldn't have picked it up. Instead, I've written it such that you only need to read a little to know *what to do next in your current situation and why*, without imposing specific choices on you.

The book provides just enough theory to inform your actions. It includes dozens of real-world examples from clients and leaders to inspire you. And, its guidance empowers you to act effectively *in your context*. You can download free supplementary resources, such as handy summaries and self-assessment questionnaires, from the book's companion website, DeliverBetterResultsBook.com. To dive much deeper into certain topics, you'll find some of the best references I know in the "Further Reading" appendix. You'll also find a list of questions for initial discussions with fellow improvement leaders.

I hope this book helps you navigate your improvement journey effectively and efficiently. I look forward to hearing about both your successes and challenges. You can reach me at gbroza@3PVantage.com.

Gil Broza, Toronto, 2023

READ THIS FIRST

If a colleague has suggested you read this book but you're short on time, read Chapter 1. You'll discover a practical model for improving your organization's value delivery, assess its level of fitness for purpose, and get an executive summary of what to do now to level up.

If you're looking for more, read Chapter 1 and then choose from the following options depending on how deep you want to go. What is your goal?

"I want to understand what specifically we need to do now."

From Chapters 5-8, read the one that corresponds to your system's current level to study the strategies for going up one level.

"I want to understand what specifically we need to do now _and_ what will maximize our chances of success."

First, read Chapters 2-3 to discover the leadership foundation that maximizes the success of improvements to the system.

Next, read Chapter 4 for a pathway to executing improvement strategies.

Then, read from Chapter 5 through to the chapter that corresponds to your system's current level to see the strategies that ought to be in place already and to study the ones that will level up the system.

"I want to understand the full picture: what specifically we need to do now, what will maximize the chances of success, and what we can expect in the future."

Read the book cover to cover.

For any of these goals, you might find the following also helpful:

- To facilitate powerful conversations and catalyze collective action, use the questions in Appendix A.

- The text includes dozens of examples of using the ideas and techniques. For a case study of using almost the entire model at a product company, read Appendix B.

- If your company is on an Agile journey or transformation, read Appendix C to learn how this book's ideas can increase its chances of success.

- To go much deeper with a certain topic or strategy than you can get from this book, follow the further-reading suggestions in Appendix D.

CHAPTER 1
THE BIG PICTURE

When you have a few quiet minutes at work — or when there's trouble — do you sometimes wonder:

"What can we do to deliver better results?"

Perhaps you're worried that your products or solutions don't meet customer and business needs as well as they should. Or, you're frustrated that despite the team's hard work, they keep falling behind, and the business needles aren't moving enough. Or, things are okay, but you can tell that there's a lot of untapped potential.

And so, you might consider upgrading processes, adopting better tools, or restructuring teams. You might also wish to get better at your own role and responsibilities — to better lead people, evolve products, design software, coach teams, and so on. To achieve the impact you're looking for, the following three matters are critical:

1. Improvement efforts should focus on the entire system of value delivery.

There's an area of your company that creates technological products and solutions for the benefit of the company's customers. The benefit is direct if the customers are the technology's users, and it's indirect if fellow colleagues use the technology.

That area is an entire *system*. It comprises the team members, management, and ways of working involved in conceiving, making, and delivering the technology. As such, changes in one part may impact other parts or be offset by their behavior, and may not improve the whole. For example:

- Starting to run product experiments will be short-lived if management always requires detailed, months-out commitments and plans.

- Releasing product updates more frequently may increase business risks if the code is sometimes unsafe.

- Abolishing meetings in the name of productivity may reduce the quality of planning decisions.

It's the results of the system — not what its parts do — that matter to customers and the business. Therefore, delivering better results requires coordinated and aligned changes across the system.

For many companies, that's a challenge: they don't manage this area as a system but as several independent parts such as Product and Engineering or Business team and IT team. It also doesn't help that as an industry, we don't have a single, unambiguous name for it. Think about other company systems, such as Sales, Finance, and HR; from their names, you know immediately who and what they include. Not this one. Many professionals refer to it as Product Development, which some others interpret as only the coding and testing part. Others refer to it as Technology, Value Stream, Project/Product Pipeline, or Software Delivery Operations, all of which may be susceptible to limiting associations and interpretations. Perhaps you have a different name for it. In this book, I'll refer to it as "value delivery system," or "system" for short.

2. A model or theory should guide your system improvement choices.

It's not enough to set improvement objectives or to have frequent retrospectives. You need a model or theory of what improvement looks like and what changes will achieve it. In the worlds of product development and solution delivery, several rather different models exist, each with its advantages and disadvantages. Some, such as Scrum and its scaled versions, minimally implement a particular philosophy (Agile, in this case) and are silent on various system-level matters. Others, such as SAFe, prescribe a specific target state for the system that may not be ideal for your particular company. And other models, such as the Theory of Constraints, suggest principles and actions for gradual improvement, but it's hard to know how the system would turn out afterwards.

3. A broad coalition of leaders should be supporting the changes.

Conceiving, making, and delivering value via technology is anything but straightforward and routine. In almost every company, it involves many interdependent people working hard to solve other people's problems within a complex and ever-shifting organizational and business context. Don't try making changes all on your own; to achieve real and sustainable improvement, collaborate with leaders from across the system. You need a coalition of leaders that, together, can:

- Overcome the organization's inertia, self-imposed constraints, and cultural barriers.
- Influence people, who have different world views, accountabilities, and concerns, to align to a set of choices so they may achieve shared success.
- Build environments where *people* — not so-called *resources* — show up and work together at their best.

FITNESS FOR PURPOSE

In thinking of value delivery as the product of a system, I've found it helpful to consider the system's **fitness for purpose**: how well it helps the company achieve its mission and objectives. By making your system more fit for its purpose, you'll deliver better results.

Having supported improvements in dozens of such real-world systems and studied many others, I've noticed that fitness for purpose generally corresponds to one of the following five progressively better levels. It's the same five whether the system is product-oriented or project-oriented, plan-driven or agile, based on a familiar framework or home-grown:

Level 1: the system has some successes, but is unable to contribute adequately to achieving company objectives.

Level 2: the system contributes to achieving company objectives, but neither effectively nor efficiently enough. (Effective: doing the right thing, solving the right problem, achieving the intended goal. Efficient: doing so with minimal waste of time, effort, resources, money, goodwill, etc.)

Level 3: the system's results are satisfactory, but fully dependent on a few people who make all the high-impact decisions.

Level 4: the system is effective and efficient, but slower to achieve major outcomes than it needs to be.

Level 5: the system produces all the results the company needs from it.

Systems that achieve great fitness get there one level at a time. They don't transform in one go into Level 5 systems: that's much more change than people can handle, even if the target state is clearly understood and communicated. In this book, we focus on going up just one level at a time, which isn't trivial either. It may take months and may be rocky, even in ideal conditions; some backsliding is not unusual.

While you might be keen (or pressed) to improve your system and deliver better results, you might also be experiencing a conflict. Amid the demand and flux of business, there never seems to be a good time to make changes. And when you do contemplate changes, so much advice on improving value delivery is available these days, it quickly gets overwhelming. At the same time, maintaining the status quo involves costs and risks.

This begs the question: What's an efficient way to level up reliably?

I've found that given a system's current fitness level, **two or three specific cross-system strategies will move it up one level effectively, efficiently, and sustainably.** In total, there are ten of these incremental and sequential strategies for moving from low to high fitness — from Level 1 to 5. They apply to all systems, though naturally they need to be customized to each system's parameters and unique context.

In this chapter, you'll determine the scope of your system, assess its current fitness, and learn briefly about the strategies that will take it to the next level. In the rest of the book, you'll learn about the foundation of leadership that makes these strategies effective and sustainable, and dive deep into each one. All of this, taken together, forms a model I've developed called **SQUARE** (because it's designed to be **S**imple, **QUA**litative, and **RE**lative).

DETERMINE THE SCOPE OF YOUR VALUE DELIVERY SYSTEM

Before you start applying this book's guidance to your system, make yourself a clear mental picture of its scope — who and what it includes. Use the following perspectives to think about it.

- **People and work:** The system includes all the individual contributors *and managers* involved in the product/solution from idea to delivery, their interactions, their work, and their methods and tools for getting work done. Its people — employees, contractors, vendor staff — may work on different teams and report to different managers (not only in technology), but they're all interdependent and necessary for conceiving, making, and delivering a complete product. That product matters to external users and customers, and/or to internal people whose work benefits external customers.

- **Parts:** The system is likely made up of parts. For example, if you work on a product line in a tech company, the parts are likely to be product management, design, engineering, and delivery, among others. If you develop software for internal purposes, the system is the equivalent in terms of IT and their business partners. If your company provides software services to other companies, the parts are development, analysis, project management, account management, client representatives, and others. Your company *might be used to managing all these parts separately* — perhaps as functions — but none of them can achieve customer and user outcomes and move business needles on their own; the system does that through all its parts working together.

- **Boundaries:** The system is a distinct subset of the company. A lot of people may care about the product/solution — or even suffer if it's poor — but unless they have some influence or control over its evolution, they are not part of the system that makes it. This is the situation, for example, in some companies with respect to marketing, HR, and customer support; in others, representatives of these functions have some influence over product choices, and are therefore part of the system.

- **Multiple systems:** Your company may have multiple value delivery systems (which might intersect somewhat). For example, in some companies, one system's aim is to explore new opportunities, and another's aim is to exploit existing opportunities. Apply this book's guidance to each one separately.

For an additional perspective, imagine that the product is a movie. What and who would the credit roll include?

Example: A company developing a marketplace in the mobile app space had two systems. One focused on the company's own app for mobile users, their engagement and retention, monetization, and app discovery. The other focused on providers of marketplace apps, ad and bidding tools for them, fraud, and more. Each system included several teams, every team consisting of front-end and back-end developers, testers, product managers, data scientists, and data analysts as their mission required. Each system also included team leads, managers, and directors. Three senior leaders were in both systems: the heads of engineering, product, and data. The CEO and the COO operated outside both systems: they did not control the workings of either one, though their decisions naturally affected the choices that system leaders made.

ASSESS YOUR SYSTEM'S CURRENT FITNESS FOR PURPOSE

The fitness for purpose of a value delivery system is how well it helps the company achieve its mission and objectives. This is a *relative* concept, since the mission and objectives vary from company to company. SQUARE defines six aspects of system fitness and a simple, qualitative way for rating them and subsequently assessing the system's fitness level.

> For an analogy, think about physical fitness. If there were some universal, absolute scale for measuring a person's fitness, yours would likely be a fraction of that of an athlete who trains daily for the Olympics. However, the *purpose* or goal for which you need fitness may be very different from the Olympian's: enjoy runs in the park, volunteer as a firefighter, or climb mountains. And then, consider the *aspects* of physical fitness, such as strength, speed, endurance,

and agility. Each of these aspects matters differently given the purpose.

To rate how your system does on each aspect, you'll work through the same three questions: what's the practical and relevant optimum for that aspect? What's the current state? How is the current state relative to its optimum? I recommend you write down your answers, at least to the third question. I've provided real-world examples for rating each aspect, as well as two examples of complete assessments. That's why this section ended up rather long!

As you'll see, this assessment is subjective. Try to be neutral, but critical; fair, but not harsh. Base your answers on actual results and behaviors, not on how people talk about them. If you struggle with a question, consider this angle: how would an independent outsider, who knows your system well, answer it?

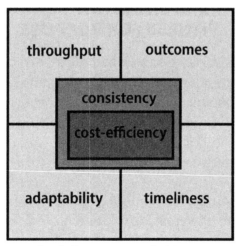

The six fitness aspects in SQUARE

Throughput

The first fitness aspect is **throughput**: the amount of usable product/solution delivered by the system in short spans of time. (Note: *usable,* not *useful.* We'll get to useful in a moment.)

Question 1: What's your system's *optimum* throughput?

In other words, what is the throughput like when the system is most fit for its purpose? What throughput (as defined here) would best serve the customers and the company?

The **optimum** must be **practical**. The system operates in a specific business and technology landscape with constraints and obligations. Even with ample time and funds, there's a limit to what would be practical.

The optimum must also be **relevant**. Even if you draw inspiration from industry stars, what throughput would *matter* most to your users? What throughput would have the best net effect on the system itself, for instance in terms of risk, learning, or adaptation?

The optimum doesn't have to be extreme. Keep in mind too that in technology development, more output (features, redesigns, enhancements) doesn't always equate to higher value or better quality.

If you're struggling to determine the optimum, try this. Given what you know of the industry, consider what the ideal throughput would be for a company like yours. Then dial it down based on your system's constraints: culture, budget, staffing, regulations, technology, etc.

Question 2: What's the system's *current* throughput?

Consider the last few months. The system's throughput would have varied over that time and across teams, so think about its average. A rough idea will do; no need for a precise answer.

Question 3: How is the current throughput *relative* to its optimum?

Rate the current throughput as follows:

- If it's far enough from the optimum that it is (or should be) a constant point of concern for management and stakeholders, rate it as "**far**."
- If it's near the optimum enough that it's not an issue (it's good enough), rate it as "**near**."

- If it's neither near nor far, rate it as "**midway**."

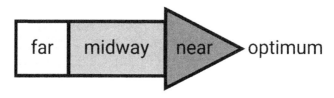

Examples:

- At a company that made a 3D visualization product, monthly releases would have been practical and most valuable. However, releases were done only every six months (at least), which wasn't good enough for the company's needs. Throughput was "far."

- A team working for a university was responsible for an established product for researchers. The team released small enhancements every week, which was just right both for them and for their customers, so throughput was "near."

- At a company that built software for product management, the development of new features took longer than desired (due to team size and aging infrastructure), but not so long as to be a constant problem, so throughput was "midway."

Note: If the product/solution hasn't had its first release yet, base the optimum (for this aspect and subsequent ones) on what's ideal for bringing it to customers for the first time. For instance, say that four months ago you started developing a large new product, and it was ideal to ship an early-adopter first version within a year. Also, say that the optimum throughput is that every two weeks, more basic functionality is completed, because that reduces risk. If that's in fact happening, throughput would be "near." However, if the teams are still debating the architecture and not validating it, throughput could be "far."

Outcomes

The second fitness aspect is **outcomes**: the system's achievement of valuable customer and business outcomes — solving problems, addressing needs, achieving goals, seizing opportunities — both large and small. This aspect also covers the matter of product/solution quality, since quality — as the customers/users see it — is what makes the achieved outcomes particularly valuable to them.

Work through the same three questions as before, this time applying them to the system's achievement of outcomes:

1. What's the practical and relevant optimum?

2. How does the system currently perform?

3. How is the current performance relative to its optimum — far, near, midway?

Examples:

- At a financial institution that was modernizing its self-serve investment platform, the teams sequenced and evolved features based on data-driven analyses of user journeys; outcomes were "near."

- At a retailer undergoing a digital transformation, teams regularly started, changed, and abandoned features, because management couldn't decide which ones would matter the most. Outcomes were "far."

- At an educational game maker, teams regularly delivered useful features (so, outcomes weren't "far"). However, based on business metrics, those were not always the best features to work on. Therefore, outcomes weren't "near" either; they were "midway."

As with throughput, you might notice differences across teams. For example, one product manager might focus her energy on outcomes and validating hypotheses, while other product managers focus primarily on populating backlogs with features. Think about the *entire* system's achievement of valuable outcomes.

Timeliness

The third fitness aspect is **timeliness**: the system's delivery of outcome-producing results when they're still valuable enough. This isn't about hitting company-determined deadlines; rather, it's in the eyes of the customers/users (who might be internal): by the time they receive updates or solutions that address their outcomes, how valuable are they?

Now work through the three questions:

1. What's the system's optimum for timeliness? Remember that it should be practical and relevant.

2. What's the current performance with respect to timeliness?

3. How is the current performance on timeliness relative to its optimum — far, near, midway?

Examples:

- In addition to regularly enhancing its digital products, a large media corporation had to customize them for major world events. The teams delivered enhancements on good schedules and their customizations were always ready for the events; timeliness was "near."

- A company had a product for connecting people, but its technology and UI were quickly getting obsolete. Three teams were busy rewriting them to current standards and expectations, but their progress was much slower than needed (due to various technical and leadership reasons) and the initial launch kept being pushed out by months. Timeliness was "far."

- The financial institution mentioned earlier deployed a bare-bones version of its new investment platform and then added features gradually. Customers didn't have to wait ages to experience its benefits, but the development of most features took a long time. Therefore, timeliness was "midway."

Adaptability

The fourth fitness aspect is **adaptability**: the ease and speed at which *both the system and its product* adapt to important changes. Changes may be due to internal choice or to external conditions, and adaptations may not necessarily be net positive.

Work through the three questions:

1. What's the optimum adaptability for both the system and its product? Its relevance is particularly important: the world moves fast these days, but not equally for everyone.

2. What's the current state of adaptability?

3. How is the current adaptability relative to its optimum — far, near, midway?

Examples:

- The university team noted earlier kept a small roadmap of features, which they reviewed frequently and adjusted as needed. The product's architecture was already proven, and changing features was relatively easy. Therefore, adaptability was "near."

- The company that made the 3D visualization product used to make big annual plans, which were hard to change. As well, the teams couldn't change the product quickly and safely for various technical reasons. Adaptability was therefore "far." After some coaching, management moved to six-month roadmaps of sequenced outcomes (with suggested but not binding dates), and the system's adaptability changed to "midway."

These four aspects are the foundational ones, because the next two "go meta": each one relates to the previous ones.

Consistency

The fifth fitness aspect is **consistency**: the system's continued achievement of its throughput, outcomes, timeliness, and adaptability. Naturally, it varies from week to week and from month to month; the lower the range of variation, the higher the consistency.

Repeat the three questions, this time for consistency:

1. What's the optimum?

2. What's the current state? Your answer here should reflect the system's normal and sustainable operation, so if it's recently been in a short crunch mode, base your answer on how things were before it.

3. How is the current state of consistency relative to its optimum?

Examples:

- At the company that was rewriting its product for connecting people, the new version's features, design, and architecture were constantly in flux. Some sprints the teams delivered useful features, and the next sprint they were told to change them. Sometimes the product seemed to be getting close to market-readiness, and then it wasn't. Consistency was "far."

- The media corporation mentioned earlier had an appropriate balance of planning and adaptation, and teams regularly built and delivered useful features. Consistency was "near."

- At an investment company, business people pop-
  ulated large backlogs that teams then processed in
  sprints. Throughput and timeliness were usually
  "midway," whereas outcomes and adaptability
  were sometimes "far," sometimes "midway." On
  the whole, consistency was "midway."

Cost-efficiency

The sixth fitness aspect is **cost-efficiency**: the efficiency
of achieving the system's current throughput, outcomes,
timeliness, adaptability, and consistency for the money spent.
It aggregates everything paid to employees, contractors, and
providers to make the system produce its effects on these five
aspects over time. That includes costs for new development,
maintenance, process administration, tools, licenses and
services, onboarding and training, and more.

One last time for the three questions:

1. What's the optimum? Be careful here: though every
   company can always cut some costs — and it might
   be forced to by external conditions — that doesn't
   mean it's inefficient *for the effects it's producing*.
   Furthermore, some kinds of cost-cutting may
   actually compromise the system's performance.

2. What's the current state?

3. How is the current state relative to its optimum?

Examples:

- At the educational game maker, teams had great
  throughput and adaptability and they did well on
  the other three aspects. However, everything was
  planned afresh every quarter, which often resulted
  in throwing away previous-quarter work that
  wasn't yet releasable. Cost-efficiency was "far."

- At the company that built software for product management, the costs were right for the system's performance. Cost-efficiency was "near."

- At the investment company, cost-efficiency was "midway": the system was right-sized for its needs and accomplishments, but it relied on many contractors and the process was heavy.

Here are two examples of complete assessments:

1. Company A, a fast-growing tech startup, had five Scrum teams working in two-week cycles, serving both public users and an internal services organization. The teams regularly made good progress, but the company needed more for its growth targets, so Throughput was "midway." Outcomes were also "midway": although product backlogs were generally prioritized by value, management was frequently nervous about the choices made. Delivery of complete and customer-meaningful features generally took long enough to rate Timeliness as "far." Changing direction in the product and adjusting the way of working weren't painful, but they weren't always easy either, making Adaptability "midway." The support from Product and Engineering directors enabled the teams to keep a good rhythm, making Consistency "near." Cost-efficiency was "midway," mostly due to the type and extent of technical debt.

2. Company B was a veteran provider of services to diverse public sector organizations. About 70 people in a digital solutions department worked on multiple customer-specific and platform-enhancement projects. The high number of concurrent projects and extensive matrixing of people resulted in a lot of late deliveries and escalations; Timeliness was "far." Throughput was also "far": although project teams nominally worked in sprints, they avoided releasing code frequently because it was hard to ensure quality. The products fulfilled their users' goals minimally and usability was basic, making Outcomes "midway." Changing or extending current products (such as due to new contracts or laws) was hard but not a common occurrence, so Adaptability was "midway." Consistency was "far": It was impossible to know whether the next month was going to go well or not. Even though the department was kept small and the teams were fully loaded all the time, the overhead of constantly coordinating and redirecting staff meant cost-efficiency was not "near" but "midway."

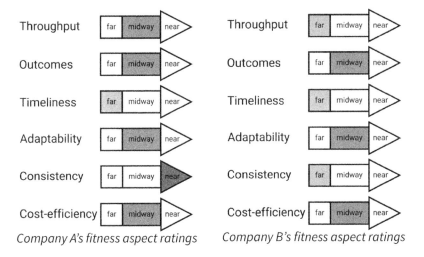

Company A's fitness aspect ratings   Company B's fitness aspect ratings

Having produced your ratings for all six aspects, I suggest you double-check them:

- For each aspect, did you think of it as defined here and rate it independently of the other ones? For example, if you thought "We deploy product releases twice a year, but we should deploy much more frequently than that," throughput can be "far" while consistency is "near" (and the system might be quite cost-efficient for its release cadence).

- If your analysis revealed that the system optimizes for some aspects at the expense of others, that's useful information — it doesn't mean you've rated them incorrectly. In a common example, a system that changes its direction and focus excessively may rate highly on adaptability but poorly on cost-efficiency due to all the abandoned work.

Consider inviting fellow leaders to perform this assessment independently, and then meet to compare your ratings. If theirs are similar to yours, that's a good indicator of alignment. If the ratings differ materially, ask everyone to articulate their views of the aspects' optimums and then of the current state; remember that the optimums need to be both practical and relevant. Either scenario will make for insightful discussions.

Now, calculate the level of your system's fitness for purpose:

1. Convert each rating to a numeric value as follows: far = 1, midway = 2, near = 3.

2. Sum up the numbers to produce the **raw fitness score**, which should be between 6 and 18. (Note: This is a simple sum. Don't prorate the ratings or assign a weight to each aspect.)

3. Find your system's fitness level in the following table:

LEVEL 1	LEVEL 2	LEVEL 3	LEVEL 4	LEVEL 5
6-8	9-11	12-13	14-16	17-18

Keep a record of your six ratings and the raw fitness score, so you can discuss them with colleagues and track changes over time. However, the level you've just calculated will be enough for knowing which improvement strategies to employ.

If the level is lower than you'd like it to be, take heart. Acknowledge the successes and positives in your journey so far, and read on to discover what will help you deliver better results.

SUPPLEMENTARY RESOURCE: Download "Fitness for Purpose Self-Assessment Questionnaire" (the above assessment in questionnaire format) from the book's companion website, DeliverBetterResultsBook.com.

HOW TO IMPROVE FITNESS

If you've rated an aspect or two as "far" or "midway," you might be thinking at this point: "Why don't we just put all our efforts toward fixing that?" For example, if outcomes are not great, our product managers and designers can run more experiments; if timeliness is poor, let's double down on correct estimation, detailed release and sprint planning, and frequent status checks.

Doing this may not actually produce the result you hope for. The reason, which Chapter 2 explains in much more detail, is that you're dealing with a complex system. Every change requires certain system-level readiness, changes in one part affect other parts, and improving one aspect may compromise another. To use the aforementioned examples:

- Running experiments regularly takes more than product thinking and a technical infrastructure. Leadership's approach to making product/solution commitments, planning, and even managing employee performance can make or break experimentation.

- Trying to make team planning and estimation more correct requires the teams to be effectively staffed for their mandate and to not be overwhelmed by many competing priorities. It may also reduce adaptability and cost-efficiency.

SQUARE's ten strategies don't target individual aspects or prescribe a process. Instead, *each strategy makes specific, principled changes to the* **way of working** *of the whole system*: how people engage with each other, decide what to work on, make commitments, plan activities, make choices while working, and deliver value. That improves all fitness aspects, though to different extents.

These strategies are **sequential** and **incremental**. I've found this to be practical, sustainable, and respectful of human systems' appetite and tolerance for change. If your organization is contemplating a "transformation," these strategies are an effective way to execute it gradually. Using even one of the strategies indicated for your system's current level will help you deliver better results; you don't have to be pursuing perfection.

Sequential: Implement the strategies in the sequence given and don't jump ahead. For instance, if your system is at Level 2, implement only that level's strategies and don't worry about those for Levels 3 or 4. Applying the later-level ones now would either not improve fitness much or be too difficult to pull off. Moreover, it would mean *a lot* of simultaneous change, and a possible distraction from the strategies that do apply now. Just keep the progression in mind so you don't undermine it inadvertently.

Incremental: To move from one level to the next, you need to execute only two or three strategies to a point where their adjustments are sustained and their effects are real. Expect that to take considerable time and effort! With supportive leadership, appetite and tolerance for change, and expert guidance, you'll minimize the time and be able to execute them in close succession.

Whatever your system's level, and whether you're currently trying to improve it or waiting for the right opportunity, **make sure to keep the lower-level strategies in play**. That should be easy if you've been following the book's advice since Level 1. However, if your system is at a higher level and you're encountering SQUARE for the first time, read up on the lower-level strategies and be sure they're being applied effectively. That is critical both for maintaining the current fitness and, if you're actively trying to level up, for getting maximum benefit from the new strategies.

To be effective, these strategies require a **foundation**: intentional leadership that actively builds and protects an explicit culture and way of working throughout the system. Chapters 2 and 3 explain and provide guidance for the specifics of that foundation.

Lastly, be aware that your system always faces multiple risks to its continuing performance and fitness. At each level, the highest risk is different, and though the risks from lower levels have likely been mitigated by the execution of those levels' strategies, they are still present.

THE 10 STRATEGIES FOR LEVELING UP

This section provides a brief summary of each level and its highest risk and then a one-paragraph description for each of its strategies for leveling up. It also provides advice for remaining at Level 5. Chapter 4 describes a pathway to follow when applying a strategy, and the subsequent chapters provide detailed guidance for each one.

It's important that you read the following subsections all the way from Level 1 to your system's current level. Also, if your system's raw fitness score is at the top end of the corresponding level (for instance, a raw score of 11 is at the top end of Level 2), be sure to read the next level — it's coming up soon.

Remember that the scope of application of each strategy is the entire system as you identified it earlier — not a single function or team and not the whole company either.

Progressing from Level 1 to 2

At this level, the system is unable to contribute adequately to achieving company objectives. The team works, sometimes very hard, and they have some successes. But on the whole, their deliverables fall short of what the business needs.

Often, the main culprit appears to be the team's process. That might be correct, but there's usually a deeper problem at the portfolio level: too many big-ticket items (projects, features, initiatives, etc.) are in flight or about to be. Various stakeholders, trying to accomplish their objectives, push work into the system and all of it fights for attention. The team tries to satisfy all the demand. Management spends considerable effort on prioritization, coordination, and escalations, but the system can't keep up.

This is usually a tense situation, because people — competent and dedicated as they are — feel that they can't succeed. *The highest risk to the system is that the key people who keep it operational may decide to leave.*

Strategy 1a: Manage the project portfolio with greater strategic control over committed and in-progress items.

Limit, choose strategically, and properly frame all portfolio items. (A portfolio item may be a feature, feature set, "epic," technical initiative, experiment, maintenance project — something big enough to make a demonstrable difference to the customers/users and the company.) Placing self-imposed limits on the number of portfolio items will clear some of the logjam and enable the system to get more work to a deliverable state more often. Strategically prioritizing the exact items to work on will further improve the system's results. This strategy requires real accountability from the decision-makers, since their choices — and how frequently their choices change — have a large effect on effort, focus, and complexity, and therefore on company results. As well, this strategy often requires the influence and involvement of very senior people, because it's hard to say "no" or "not yet" to important work, especially when it's tied to managers' objectives.

Strategy 1b: Design the way of working based on what matters most for achieving the mission and objectives.

The operating model needs to be capable of producing the system's intended results. Rather than adopt a favorite/familiar/popular model and try to make it work in your context, design yours intentionally and explicitly. Start by getting leader alignment and consensus about what the system needs to be like if it's highly fit for its purpose. From there, work together to answer these questions: What is vital for the system to deliver the right product/solution to the right customer at the right time, and why do we choose the answers we do? Use the answers to determine the way of working. For example, if frequent delivery and high adaptability are vital for product success, you'll probably organize around semi-autonomous teams working in flow or sprints.

Progressing from Level 2 to 3

A Level 2 system addresses the needs of customers, stakeholders, and management but not effectively and efficiently enough. As a result, some of those needs produce interference, unplanned work, scope creep, frequent priority changes, escalations, and aborted work. These disruptions are *the highest risk to the system's continued fitness: the structure and process, which are already not optimal, are constantly under threat.* Often, this triggers process patches and restructurings that satisfy a few imperatives at the expense of overall system fitness, risking a drop to Level 1.

Strategy 2a: Establish clear and appropriate decision-making.

Whether you've organically evolved your way of working or adopted off-the-shelf process frameworks, chances are there's a gap: who makes some decisions, when, and how is unclear, inconsistent, or not fully defined. Closing this gap is a necessary, though not sufficient, condition of both effectiveness and efficiency. To do that, review every type of high-impact, product-affecting decision, and gain clarity and acceptance on which individuals or groups make it and how. Use the system's intended values and principles, as determined in Level 1 and perhaps refined since then, to guide the choice for each decision. For example, if the system operates according to Agile values, many decisions would likely be made collaboratively by cross-functional groups; if it operates in a top-down functional model, many decisions would likely be made only by functional and project managers.

> **Terminology note:** I define "Agile" as any way of working that is *congruent with the spirit* of the Agile Manifesto. It may factor in modern insights and apply across more kinds of work than software development.

Strategy 2b: Stabilize the system.

Create an acceptable and sustainable balance between the variable demand that the system receives and the supply it produces. Be wary of common practices that may help some, but when executed regularly compromise various fitness aspects: making complete detailed plans, preparing precise estimates, maximizing people's utilization, and working long hours. Instead, use principles and tactics that improve the flow of work. Capture all the work in a rich visual form; that will help you finish what's started, reduce unplanned work, and deal promptly with bottlenecks and high-variability delays. Prevent "clogging the pipe" by constraining work intake, breaking work down, and keeping spare capacity. On the human front, cultivate learner safety, increase trust, and enable people to contribute outside narrow specialties. Collect process data, but use it only for system improvement; be careful not to let data collection, analysis, and subsequent actions compromise psychological safety and trust.

Progressing from Level 3 to 4

The typical Level 3 system contributes satisfactorily to the achievement of company objectives. Usually, only one or two of the six fitness aspects are of ongoing concern, while one or two others are close enough to their optimum. If the operational model is based on short cycles, the teams churn out working product on a rather even keel; if it's more project- or date-driven, teams generally hit their dates.

Look closely, and you'll notice why the system is only at Level 3: its results are fully dependent on a few people who make all the high-impact decisions. Typically, those folks are product leads, architects or senior individual contributors, and middle managers — and they don't act as a team. Some might be considered "heroes." Two unvoiced assumptions are shared throughout the system and explain a lot about it: the planned work equals the right work, and the potential improvement gains from collaboration aren't worth the time.

The overweighting of those few people in decisions about the work, and the teams' unwavering cadence of delivery, lead to disengagement. Team members, instead of tapping into their creativity, feel like cogs in a machine — fully loaded "resources" that check tasks off, disconnected from the mission and/or their customers. The machine, however, is optimized a certain way, and has low capacity to adapt to big changes. *The highest risk to the system's fitness is chaos and breakdown due to big changes.* Sometimes, the key people mentioned above are the only barrier to the chaos.

These phenomena may create a vicious cycle: the less team members engage (the more they "just do the work"), the more the decision-makers operate in isolation. Such systems are likely to retreat to Level 2 if enough key people leave.

Strategy 3a: Increase contributor safety, real teamwork, and collaboration.

This multi-component strategy sits squarely on the human side of the system. Work with leaders on creating contributor safety, one side of which is the safety to engage where others are involved: to offer different perspectives, to take initiative, to deliver bad news. For the other side of safety, upgrade the process so folks may do their work without fear of failure or trouble. Check if teams are really teams or only workgroups; if it's the latter, find and address the root causes that real teamwork hasn't materialized. Look for situations that would benefit from collaboration, and create the conditions that make collaboration possible and welcome both within teams and across the system. By unleashing people's potential and synergy, this strategy mitigates the key-person risk and improves results and resilience. It's also an enabler of the next two.

Strategy 3b: Defer commitments and increase release frequency while controlling costs.

In choosing what work to do, the system looks ahead to different horizons, for example 12-24-month roadmaps, 3-6-month releases, and 2-week touchpoints. It makes commitments whose nature and extent vary by horizon. The first component of this strategy is to commit to less and plan in less detail for the longer horizons. The second component, which will now be easier, is to increase the frequency of releasing product/solution updates. As you do all this, prevent two important costs from rising too much: the cost of change (that is, the affordability of likely future adaptations) and process costs (planning, coordinating, releasing, etc.). Implement this strategy gradually because commitments and release frequency affect other systems in the company and are affected by them, and therefore require greater alignment and partnership with all those systems' leaders. This strategy will result in risk reduction, earlier value to customers, easier pivoting, less wasted work, and greater resilience to big changes.

Strategy 3c: Engage teams meaningfully, collaboratively, and efficiently in planning.

People in your system engage in a lot of planning: all the activities that lead to commitments, what they encompass, and how the system will act on them. Examples abound: product discovery, solution design, work breakdown, release and sprint planning, scheduling, and migration planning. Improve each activity's output by engaging the relevant teams and experts (in other words, not only the decision-makers or managers). Experiment with ways for them to contribute to the planning as meaningfully, collaboratively, and efficiently as possible. Much of this will happen in meetings; make them worth having and facilitate them well. As a result of this strategy, the system may produce better outcomes, achieve higher throughput (by reducing unnecessary work), deliver more-timely results (by reducing delays), and respond better to events.

Progressing from Level 4 to 5

The typical Level 4 system is both appropriately adaptive and a reliable producer of deliverables. Both staff and management see it as a good place to work. While on a tactical level there seems to be healthy progress, a higher-level view reveals why the system is not at Level 5: it struggles to pull off "big work" of strategic value to customers and the company, such as integrating an acquisition, re-platforming, or supporting new customer journeys. It succeeds eventually, but it's slower than the company needs it to be. Therefore, *the highest risk to the system is a breakdown of process and good habits due to loss of stakeholders' trust and/or management's patience.*

Strategy 4a: Expand team ownership of major outcomes.

Increase teams' ownership as much as necessary and possible for the system's optimal fitness. Enable teams to experiment with their own ideas for better ways of working that would benefit the whole system; this might include re-teaming or starting up guilds and temporary task forces. Give them a greater say over identifying and sequencing major outcomes and how to achieve them. That will counteract the tendency to concentrate "big-work thinking" in the hands of a select few, who then present final-looking but too-big requirements to the technical teams. The extra brainpower and thought diversity will open up options for better solutions, while the increased participation will encourage the teams to put more heart and energy into work and reduce attrition.

Strategy 4b: Improve the inputs to decisions and the decision-making processes.

The previous strategies would have improved the quality of decisions made about the system and the product. However, some decisions still end up producing negative *actual* outcomes, sabotaging the *intended* positive ones and creating other problems (which may be hard to trace back to the decision). Improve the inputs to decisions by better understanding the customers (both external and internal), collecting feedback, and running tests, studies, and experiments. Improve decision-making processes by considering both intended and actual outcomes, using system thinking, and accounting for the cost of change. Enable your people to do all this by cultivating humility and challenger safety, reframing decisions as bets, and making decisions collaboratively.

Strategy 4c: Reduce the technical cost of change.

Your system and product/solution undergo change all the time, and it costs you. By implementing the strategies for Levels 1-3, you've been controlling the cost of change on several fronts except one: how much the system spends on technical modifications to the product. Some of those are infrequent, such as modernization, enhancing once-optimal solutions that no longer are, and correcting problematic past choices. Others are made practically every day as part of regular development (even if the team is building brand-new features). To the extent the time spent on all this change exceeds its ideal minimum, it diminishes the system's fitness. This strategy has two components. One: reduce the cost of the likeliest changes to *existing* parts of the product by making it cheaper, easier, and safer to work with those parts. Two, develop *new* parts in a way that makes the likeliest changes affordable. Day to day, that requires following technical agility principles such as rapid feedback, small and safe steps, and clean code. To make this strategy possible, three parties — development, product/business, and management — need to make an intentional, explicit, and mutual commitment to investing in the system this way.

Remaining at Level 5

A Level 5 system is uncommon: all fitness aspects are close enough to their optimum that there's rarely any issue. It takes years of deliberate leadership to cultivate such a way of working and the strong culture that enables it. Keep yours at Level 5 by ensuring that the ten strategies mentioned earlier continue to be in play throughout the system.

Despite the system's great performance, its *culture* might experience friction with that of the company. At the time of writing, this friction tends to occur in systems based on philosophies such as servant leadership, agility, and Lean that operate within companies that default to hierarchical control and predictability.

The friction is usually felt at the edges of the system, where it interfaces with the rest of the company. Senior people at the edges (such as VPs and product leads) buffer the system from the friction, managing it well through trusting relationships with their colleagues outside the system. *The highest risk to this status quo is a change at the top.* A new senior leader — at the helm of the system or just above it — may try to reshape it based on their own world-view and experiences in other contexts. I'm familiar with several cases where the cultural disruption was powerful enough to undermine the implementation of the strategies and send the system back to a lower level of fitness.

Two partly overlapping actions provide some "insurance" against disruption to the system's culture. One, continue building trusting relationships with stakeholders and executives. Hopefully, by now they see your value delivery system as a critical partner (not as an internal vendor) but you shouldn't assume that results speak for themselves. Two, help leaders of other company systems be more successful. Partnering, sharing lessons learned, and teaching them what you've learned along your journey will strengthen your relationships with them; to the extent they choose to shift their culture and ways of working to resemble yours, there'll be less friction.

Summary of the Five Levels

Level	Fitness	Highest risk	Strategies for leveling up
1	Has some successes, but is unable to contribute adequately to achieving company objectives	Loss of key people	Manage the project portfolio; design the way of working
2	Contributes to achieving company objectives, but neither effectively nor efficiently enough	Excessive disruptions → setbacks	Sort out decision-making; stabilize the system
3	Results are satisfactory, but fully dependent on a few people who make all the high-impact decisions	Big changes → chaos and breakdown	Increase safety, teamwork, and collaboration; defer commitments and increase release frequency; engage teams in planning
4	Effective and efficient, but slower to achieve major outcomes than it needs to be	Loss of patience and trust → breakdown of good habits	Expand team ownership; improve decision-making; reduce the technical cost of change
5	Produces all the results the company needs from it	Change at the top → being reshaped	Build trusting relationships; help others improve their systems

SUPPLEMENTARY RESOURCE: Download "Summary of the Five Levels" from the book's companion website, DeliverBetterResultsBook.com.

FITNESS DOESN'T STAY CONSTANT

Even when you're not actively looking to level up your system's fitness for purpose, expect it to fluctuate with time. The aspects' optimums may change, for example due to shifting market needs and preferences. The aspects' current state may also change, for example if enough key people leave or take on different responsibilities, or if technologies you rely on are retired. These changes might result in a shift to the ratings; for instance, an aspect might go from "midway" (okay but not great) to "far" (a real problem). For this reason, it's helpful to recalculate the raw fitness score every now and again and watch for changes.

A familiar special case of such change is rapid growth. Scaling up is often accompanied by increased expectations for the foundational aspects' optimums. However, quickly adding many new hires may send the performance on those aspects in the wrong direction: throttling throughput, compromising outcomes, reducing timeliness, and hampering adaptability.

If your system is growing fast or if its fitness has dropped, redouble your execution of the strategies that are already in place, starting with Level 1 and working sequentially to the current level. For example, an EdTech (education technology) company at Level 4 increased headcount by 20% to support its expansion to new markets. It had to update its portfolio management to reflect the new capacity (Strategy 1a) and to ensure that the team structure was appropriate (1b); then it had to plug newly formed gaps in decision-making (2a) and stabilize the bigger system (2b); then it had to "relearn" how to defer commitments (3b). However, doing all this was much quicker than getting to Level 4 the first time around.

WHAT TO READ NEXT

You've just assessed your system's fitness level. You've also read very brief descriptions of the two or three strategies to level up and of the lower-level strategies that should already be in place. Perhaps this is enough for you to set in motion some wheels of change.

You'll find deeper descriptions of Levels 1-4, explanations of their strategies, and advice about executing them in Chapters 5-8. If you're short on time and want to know what specifically to do now, proceed to the chapter that corresponds to your system's current level. If you have a bit more time, and reading the text above made you suspect that the lower-level strategies aren't as "baked in" as they should be, read their chapters first.

If you're going to be closely involved in leading these changes, take the time to first read Chapters 2-4. They provide critical information about value delivery systems and explain the necessary leadership foundation for effectively executing the strategies.

For an example of a company using the strategies to move Product Development from Level 1 to 4 in only 10 months, read Appendix B. If your organization is currently on an "Agile journey" or formally undergoing an "Agile transformation," read Appendix C to learn how this book's ideas can increase its chances of success.

 SUPPLEMENTARY RESOURCES: Go to DeliverBetterResultsBook.com and download "Fitness for Purpose Self-Assessment Questionnaire" and "Summary of the Five Levels."

CHAPTER 2
UNDERSTANDING SYSTEMS OF VALUE DELIVERY

When you think about how product development or solution delivery is done in your company, what comes to mind?

Chances are, it's a concrete who/what/how kind of picture showing the various functions and teams, their processes and practices, management's involvement, how releases are put together, and so on. This chapter will explain additional and more conceptual perspectives, which play a crucial role in improving value delivery.

SYSTEM THINKING

Every person in the system, in the course of doing their work, makes choices. These choices often have visible local effects on the product/solution: UX designers' choices affect its usability, developers' technical decisions direct its construction, and so on. Choices also have effects beyond one's specific role, task, or deliverable. For example:

- At an infrastructure management company, UX folks regularly produced beautiful and complete designs without exploring their coding and testing implications. Developers implemented those designs fully. It usually took months to realize that some of the assumed use cases were off the mark and some of the right ones were missed.

- At a company that made factory management software, the development team evolved their Kanban board to a point where it was great for managing big features, bugs, and escalations. However, little features weren't getting appropriate attention even when product managers marked them as high priority.

- At several other companies, Engineering built a continuous delivery pipeline. They released code to production more often, but sometimes it wasn't actually safe to deploy.

In all cases (and there's no shortage of additional examples), everyone meant well. And yet, they produced negative business effects, all for the same reason: managing functions/roles and their work, and trying to improve their performance, in isolation — without consideration of impact to the system and beyond.

You already know that successful value delivery takes more than people just doing their jobs. They need to ensure continued alignment to the same goals, coordinate tasks and dependencies, sometimes help each other, and more. As you lead or support improvements to value delivery, make them more effective by basing choices on the understanding that value delivery occurs in a system.

Every system has a purpose. The purpose of the system you work in is to create technological products or solutions that help the company achieve its mission and objectives. A system also has boundaries, inputs and outputs, and a coherent organization. Most importantly for this discussion, it consists of (imperfect) parts that depend on other parts and interact with them to achieve the system's purpose. None of the parts can achieve it independently. For example, if your company develops internal-use applications, it has probably structured business analysis and software development as standalone parts, but neither of them can define and deliver complete and correct solutions entirely on their own. Even if parts are systems in their own right, their operation affects others and the system's behavior. For an analogy, consider the digestive system and its effect on the bigger system of the human body: thinking, mood, energy, and so on.

It would be so easy if value delivery were the sum of the independent contributions of its parts. To make a great product, all you'd need is for each part to do its job well. And if a part underperformed, you'd manage it more closely, maybe even switch it out for a better one (e.g., by outsourcing). Unfortunately, this mechanistic approach has not worked well for conceiving, making, and delivering software-based technology. That's because as a system, such value delivery is actually the product of the interactions of its parts.[1]

To illustrate this concept, think about the following not-uncommon example. Engineering is great: they deliver features on an adequate, reliable schedule. Product is also great: they always have ideas that solve actual user problems. Unfortunately, their ideas also result in a mess of dependencies, complexities, and special cases, but they don't realize it. Engineering staff and leaders feel unsafe to push back or to even discuss the technical ramifications of Product's choices. If both sides go on like this, the system's productivity and the software's quality will gradually decline. This is a system-level problem, which can't be solved by improving each part. They need to interact openly and honestly for better results.

The other important matter to know about value delivery systems is that they contain cause-and-effect relationships, some of which are complex (in large part because human beings are involved). Chains of relationships may form feedback loops. Some loops maintain balance in the system; they resist change. Other loops reinforce change; they're called virtuous cycles when the change is for the better and vicious cycles when the change is negative. You must account for relationships and loops to solve problems effectively.

For an example of a reinforcing loop, let's assume that the rate of delivery is less than satisfactory. The go-to solution, almost everywhere, is to hire more people. But is that the right solution? Imagine we dig deep and find that the process for work management produces more hand-offs and delays than necessary. This causes a vicious cycle: workers, wanting to not wait idly, pick up additional work, which is no better managed; partly done work piles up in people's queues, which exacerbates the waiting. If you don't fix the work management problem, hiring more people won't improve the rate of delivery as hoped, and may actually negatively affect other matters, such as quality and teamwork.

For an example of a balancing loop, consider the following scenario: the team relies on too much manual end-to-end testing to ensure product quality. Technical leaders determine that the team should write unit tests for existing code: the tests would detect and pinpoint breakage early and thus improve quality and productivity. While this idea can be a solid long-term strategy, it often has an upfront cost: developers need to spend time producing a test suite that's comprehensive enough to be useful. That reduces their capacity for new development and defect fixing. If this system is like most, it has feedback loops to quickly notice and act on a drop in capacity: metrics and status meetings reveal a slowdown, and business/product people put pressure on development, or someone complains to a higher-up that a feature is taking longer than expected. Within a couple of months, the unit-testing idea dies quietly.

The system can be challenging to deal with, as these two examples show, but it can also compound the positive effect of a seemingly simple change. Suppose your team works on a prioritized feature list (A through Z); the team regularly has five features in flight, and now you're reducing that number to three. Since A, B, and C receive greater attention in a short period of time, they move faster through the pipeline, possibly being tested and/or partially delivered earlier. As a result of the customer value delivered, feedback, and learning from those three features, management decides to invest more in B, remove E from the list, and move G up. Fast forward a few months, and your customers have received higher value (and received it sooner), because the less-impactful features didn't take time away from the more-impactful ones. And, depending on the specifics of the scenario, there may have been other positive effects, such as greater team morale, less technical debt, and less wasted planning time.

> *Terminology note:* You might have encountered (or used) two other common terms for the value delivery system concept: "value stream" and "pipeline." Both terms reflect that value creation extends before and after coding, that demand is continuous, and that capacity is real and limited. However, these terms may also connote that work products and cause-and-effect relationships flow in only one direction — downstream — even though a system's parts are more like an interconnected network. I believe that for increasing fitness, the word "system" is more likely to produce appropriate management responses.

MANAGING A SYSTEM

Via its product or solution, your system produces results: customer/user outcomes and effects on the company's business. What you manage is how the system *works*; change the way it works, and it may produce different results.

When you have clarity of the system's purpose, parts, and scope (or boundaries), you can manage its internal operation effectively. You can also pay appropriate attention to its interactions with its environment — other company systems and the company itself — even if you have limited influence over them.

Unless the system is quite small, managing it holistically can be hard. How can you break the problem down? A traditional approach is to arrange the system in functional parts (silos) with hand-offs between them, with senior people controlling who does what, when, and how. Another approach manages work as projects with specially assembled teams. The Agile approach divides the system into collaborative, cross-functional, and usually long-lived teams, each of which looks after many value creation activities. But even with this approach, which seems to simplify and decentralize system management, it remains a challenge, as the following story demonstrates.

A small company lost 90% of its tech people in 2020-21. Then, the heads of Product and Engineering rebuilt their respective teams, reaching Fitness Level 4 within a year. Although they collaborated well, there were instances of localized thinking:

- Product would write great feature descriptions, which Engineering would then develop in their entirety using a Kanban flow. The two parties never discussed evolving features strategically, or considered stopping work once enough value had been delivered.

- Given their high workload, the head of Engineering always made sure his team had high-priority work to pull, but the engineers often made calls without understanding the full picture.

- Product people didn't attend daily team meetings (standups), thinking the meetings weren't meant for them. That was a missed opportunity for sharing knowledge and making quick adjustments.

In a system that's fit for its purpose, leaders of parts facilitate the operation of their parts while collaborating with other leaders on system-wide optimization. The more-senior leaders are in charge of the system, ensuring that it "points in the right direction" in terms of the company's mission, strategy, and priorities. For that purpose, they act as a team, with clear and shared mission, values, goals, and working agreements. They collaborate with their peers elsewhere in the company on setting vision and strategy, ensuring alignment, managing constraints and dependencies, and responding to events. They review the system's operation frequently and facilitate adjustments as needed.

If a system's staff have a high level of *autonomy* or *ownership*, they — rather than management and powerful stakeholders — make many of its operational decisions. They collaborate on deliverables; everybody is aware of the work that's in flight and follows the same criteria for choosing what to do next. They clear blockages and shorten delays to the best of their abilities. **The greater the workers' ownership, the more attention management can pay to managing the system, and the likelier they are to collaborate with the workers on system improvements.**

Terminology note: Another word used in this context is *empowerment*. However, autonomy and ownership are higher standards. Autonomy is owned — built into the system — while empowerment is given (and can therefore be taken away).

WAY OF WORKING

A system *way of working* is how it turns inputs into outputs. To improve value delivery, enhance the way of working. That is the target of the ten improvement strategies in this book.

A way of working has two main parts: *mindset* and *tactics*.

In a work context, I've found it useful to define mindset as how folks make choices — that is, their attitude or approach toward work — and to model it as consisting of three main elements. The two foundational elements are values and beliefs, and they give rise to the third element, principles.

Values are what people consider most important for achieving their purpose. In the '90s, almost all software development environments valued the following the most: making early commitments, getting stuff right the first time, delivering on time and on budget, and standardization.

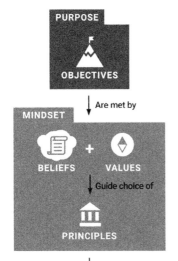

BELIEFS
What you hold to be true

VALUES
What you consider nonnegotiable,
most important, or aspirational

PRINCIPLES
Standards that guide your
choices, decisions, and actions

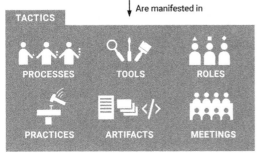

Way of working = mindset + tactics

SUPPLEMENTARY RESOURCE: Download the "Way of Working" visual
from the book's companion website, DeliverBetterResultsBook.com.

Nowadays, the four Agile values are preeminent in more
and more software development organizations: putting
people first, adaptation, early and frequent value delivery, and
customer collaboration. Many other organizations espouse
a mix of some of these and other values. A set of values is
typically small (three to five), mutually reinforcing, and
mighty: they affect *everything* about the system's operation.

Terminology note: What I refer to as values sometimes has another name, such as "core priorities."[2] Also, it is more expansive

than "cultural values," which express how people treat each other, but are silent on getting work done.

Pause here and consider: what are the few values that really drive everything in your system? (This might take you a bit to answer!)

Beliefs are people's most impactful assumptions about individuals, teams, the work, and the work's customers. Beliefs give the values context and validity, but they can be tricky: even though they sound like facts, they're really strongly held assumptions. Taken together, beliefs form a narrative or model of the world. The typical value delivery system's operation rests on a couple dozen beliefs. Here are examples of beliefs from different systems:

- We can't have all the answers up front.
- People won't do the work adequately unless they're driven, incentivized, or given deadlines.
- If everyone does their part perfectly, the product will be great.
- We're close with our customers and we think we know what they want.
- Engaged workers make happy customers. Happy customers make a successful business.

Pause again and consider: what are some of the beliefs that explain why your system works the way it does?

Based on its values and beliefs, a system operates by a set of **principles**: choices for engaging individuals and teams, doing the right work, managing the work, and delivering value over time. Principles permeate all aspects of the work, and some principles reinforce others. For instance, two Waterfall principles are "plan the work, and work the plan" and "limit change," while two Agile ones are "work in self-organizing, collaborative, cross-functional teams" and "trust people to act professionally and conscientiously."

Tactics are the documentable, teachable mechanics people use for dealing with work. "Tactics" is the umbrella term for processes, practices, roles and organizational structure, artifacts, meetings, and tool usage. Examples of tactics include development specifications, weekly status meetings, pull requests, outcome-based product roadmaps, tech leads, and QA teams.

Mindset determines people's choice of tactics and the behaviors, actions, and habits by which they execute them. For instance, if the people in system X optimize for getting deliverables right the first time, and believe that putting together a plan for achieving that is possible and useful, they will likely first plan all the work and then follow the plan. The tactics might include a project planning phase replete with detailed estimates and dependency analysis, a work breakdown structure, and weekly status meetings with team leaders. This example is characteristic of traditional project management.

In a different example, if the people in system Y value adaptation, and believe that short and meaningful feedback loops are possible, they might choose to plan and work in short cycles. They might conduct weekly meetings to discuss the team's results with stakeholders, followed by a planning meeting that takes their feedback and any new information into account. This example is characteristic of many Agile teams.

When a value or principle is ingrained — applied consistently enough, whether consciously or not — it is evident in habits and behaviors. Thus, it's possible to infer an individual's or group's actual mindset by watching their actions. That is often more reliable than asking them to articulate it.

Pause again (one last time) and make this relationship between mindset and tactics tangible with a full example from your system: "We value X, and believe Y, so we do Z." Or go the other way: "We do A because we think B and care about C."

While mindset — as a set of values, beliefs, and principles — is usually attributed to individual people, groups with a common objective may have a shared mindset that guides their collective actions. In fact, they *should* adhere to a shared, explicit one if their actions are to be coherent and aligned (even though it's guaranteed to have some inconsistencies, since those are human beings). Identifying the best mindset for the system's needs, and guiding the people to espouse it, are key responsibilities of senior leadership.

There's no single, optimal way to implement a given set of values. Rather, it depends on the beliefs and the specific organizational context. For example, some systems achieve frequent adaptation by having teams work in sprints, while others achieve it with work-in-process (WIP) limits on workflow stages; some get their best feedback from sprint review meetings with stakeholders, while others get it through one-on-one interviews. Mindset variations across a system are also fine as long as they're congruent with each other and give rise to a coherent whole.

A pension fund had eight separate systems, each consisting of a single team of IT folks and business partners. While the VP of Technology had initially meant to implement Scrum uniformly across all teams, the fund's strong "people over process" culture resulted in all eight customizing an Agile way of working differently — but for each, effectively.

The most notable example was a team developing an innovative trading scheme. Their product owner was a trader — the only money-making role at the firm — so his time was *expensive*. When they told him, "We need you for an hour every two weeks for the sprint demo, and a bit longer for planning," they were met with laughter. Asking him to write user stories and acceptance tests was equally futile. Instead, the team, comprising three developers and two BAs, met with him every day after the close of trading for a five-minute Q&A/demo. Additionally,

> the team stopped having daily standups: they sat in
> such close quarters, talking all the time, and having
> good visibility into their work's state, that they had
> no need for that daily meeting.

I can't emphasize enough **the significance of intentional and explicit values and beliefs to the design of a way of working**. Most organizations don't realize it. Instead, they determine processes and policies, and treat values as seasoning, which is backward. Fitness requires that the values come first, because they answer the question "What's important for our success?"

Mindset matters more than tactics

In the examples of systems X and Y above, the mindset is consistent (the principles support the values and agree with the beliefs) and is also congruent with the tactics. This alignment is important so that everyone knows how to act and the overall work experience is coherent — even if the values are not the optimal choice for the desired outcomes, or if some of the beliefs turn out to be false.

Suppose that to increase fitness, you adopt promising new tactics. If they largely align with the current mindset, they'll probably improve fitness after folks have had some time for learning and adjustment.

What you need to worry about is *incongruence*: mis-alignment between the new tactics and the prevailing mindset. This situation has been common in Agile trans-formations where teams start using "Agile practices" but hold on to a non-Agile mindset. For example, they conduct a daily Scrum meeting, but instead of it being a collaborative and quick team touchpoint for optimizing the next 24 hours, they run it as a status report with everyone giving updates to the manager. Or, they don't start any coding until they've received the full set of requirements and completed a developer spec.

In this situation, don't expect the new tactics to stick or to be used effectively; they won't increase fitness. That's because mindset is a lot more powerful than tactics. When there's trouble — a looming deadline, too many #1 priorities, risks to customer promises — the unchanged values will override the new tactics. You'll see that in the behaviors of team members, managers, and executives. Since the unchanged prevailing values reflect what the company wants and considers necessary for success, acting accordingly is personally safe behavior, and folks stay employed.

The other situation you need to worry about is mindset misalignment between people: inter-dependent colleagues making fundamentally different choices. This can happen within teams, for instance when some members thrive on collaboration while others always work solo. In another common scenario, the entire team genuinely adopts the Agile mindset, but their management and stakeholders keep a traditional one. For example, the team congregates every two weeks to plan the next sprint, but its contents were mostly predetermined for them weeks ago in a big project plan and there's no room for adaptability. Or, the team wants to sit in on some customer interviews, but management presses members to pull only coding tasks, in a bid to maximize "resource efficiency."

Misalignment between people occurs normally, because everyone has different ideas, preferences, and experiences when it comes to doing work. Where one person seeks and applies feedback, another moves ahead without questions. Where one believes in evolving the product or solution, another worries about surprises. If they work on the same team, there will be conflict and frustration because everyone thinks their approach is better for accomplishing the mission. However, these tensions will be hard to pinpoint and resolve, because folks' different abstract choices are not obvious when they all nominally use the same tactics, such as sprints and backlogs.

Misalignments create dysfunction that affects everyone. They confuse people, who hoped to get certain results but get others. They engender disenchantment, ill will, and blame. The system's outcomes fall short of the needed ones.

Therefore, as you apply the improvement strategies in this book, **work on both mindset and tactics** from day one. Make sure everybody agrees to abide by a common set of values and beliefs for shared success *despite personal preferences*. This is so critical, it's a keystone of one of the Level 1 strategies (explained in Chapter 5).

Formality

The goal of having a shared understanding of a coherent way of working does not imply a need for thick methodology books. Again, context matters.

Some environments value safety, predictability, and standardization due to their work context. As a result, they require a high level of process formality and rigor. Other environments value different matters more — for example, going to market early — and can get away with a lot less formality. What they *should* define clearly and unequivocally are their values, beliefs, and principles, and the expectation that the teams' tactics align with them.

> I saw an extreme case of this in 2021, at a fast-growing software company. Product Development fitness was at Level 4, but the executives thought that their Agile maturity was low. On the surface, the teams were using a mix of Scrum and Kanban that wouldn't have passed muster by the standards of either method. Some practices were loose and others were absent. However, a thoroughly people-first, team-everywhere, servant-leadership philosophy drove everything in Product Development, and their methods implemented — intentionally and explicitly — a host of Agile principles. For example:

- Their four development teams were able to work on any initiative on the roadmap. (This is an Agile ideal that I'd rarely seen implemented.)
- The teams pulled work from the roadmap based on their availability.
- They generally had low amounts of work in process even though they never had explicit numerical WIP limits.
- When I met them, they were refactoring and rewriting major parts of the code. The new code was clean and fully covered by excellent unit tests.
- They were continuously adapting their process to changing circumstances and needs.

As their tactics didn't look anything like common Agile templates, most people didn't realize how agile they actually were. But their implementation wasn't loose or uninformed; rather, it was informal and light.

People need simplicity, and they need a small set of ideas to fall back on when the methodology is silent or when there's trouble. Therefore, be careful not to make the methodology or playbook too detailed or tactical. It can never be complete enough to address every eventuality anyway. Better to spend your efforts on reinforcing principles, guidelines, and guardrails.

CULTURE

When values, beliefs, and their reinforcing behaviors, social norms, and stories persist across an organization and across time, we call that culture. Culture encompasses both our approach to people (e.g., "we respect each other" or "stay in your lane") and our general approach to work (e.g., "we're flexible" or "failure is not an option").

Culture persists through leaders' actions: what they say and don't say, do and don't do, reward and punish, welcome and resist. The less suitable the culture is to the organization's mission, the lower the ceiling on the system's potential fitness.

> In the last few years, I've recommended to a few new clients that used Scrum that they replace sprints with Kanban flow management (the reasons had to do with their contexts, constraints, and needs). My clients had similar questions and concerns about this idea, one of which stood out:
>
> "If we don't have sprints — with ceremonies, commitments, estimates, demos, and velocity — how can we make sure the teams are productive?"
>
> While Kanban offers a solid response to this concern, that didn't seem to help. What these managers were really asking was:
>
> "Without these elements, how can we be sure that team members would have the discipline and accountability to do the work?"
>
> This is usually a pivotal point in the conversation. The managers were making a certain cultural assumption without realizing it:
>
> "We need process mechanisms to control the environment, otherwise people won't work as much. Scrum provides enough control, Kanban doesn't."
>
> Think about this assumption. This isn't about Scrum or Kanban; it's about the managers' philosophy of management and their view of the staff.
>
> Those managers were *not* old-school controlling bosses. They were kind, friendly, caring, and wanting the best for their teams. At the same time, they were accountable for getting deliverables produced.

> Imagine how hard it was for them to realize that despite wanting to use empowering ways of working, they weren't fully trusting their people, relying instead on process to compel them to work. To improve matters, they had to think and act differently — and the system in which they worked had to change to enable that.

As you work to clarify and enhance the culture of the system, it must be congruent with the culture of the company, or the latter will stifle it. In a telling example that I still encounter often, product development leaders make their systems very adaptable, but their companies don't take advantage of that adaptability. Instead, with a company culture that values control and predictability, executives and stakeholders regularly expect system leaders to make *detailed* commitments for the next 6 or 12 months.

Having said that, companies and their systems change, and affect each other, over time. Culture changes too, albeit slowly. As a result, some changes might be easier or harder to make later on. Another implication is that there's no perfect end-state you can plan to achieve.

People often think of their organization's culture as intentionally designed, without realizing that some cultures are, in fact, accidental. Instead of an intentional, consistent, continuously nurtured way of being, a system (or an entire company) might espouse a hodge-podge of beliefs and values, largely a result of its growth trajectory and a rotation of managers. The culture must be coherent for improvements to be sustainable.

> When I start helping a company strategize about improving its value delivery, I conduct a present-state assessment. For part of it, I look at the stated values and the de-facto values — what the system *actually* optimizes for. There's always a gap.

> At one product company, several managers mentioned teamwork as the highest value — higher than customer orientation, delivering on time, quality, or getting a lot done. However, very little in the process or the company made this value real. In fact, on closer examination, there was no clear and consistent hierarchy of values. That meant there was no culture-backed, definite strategy for succeeding in value delivery.

Your system's fitness arises from its people's choices and actions, but those people may be different over time. While some level of turnover is normal and healthy, the culture may cause the system's turnover to be much higher. That costs money and commands considerable management attention, but more critically, it causes trouble such as delays, quality risks, knowledge loss, and engagement issues that may start a vicious cycle. All this takes away from the energy and focus leaders can dedicate to increasing fitness. If your company has a revolving door now, it may not be in a position yet to dedicate attention to increasing fitness; "stop the bleeding" at the company level first.

PEOPLE-FIRST VS. PROCESS-FIRST

Your system is made up of people. It's they who have a "way of working" to produce results for other people. The whole thing is managed and led by ... people.

These days, many companies claim to have a specific cultural value: "We put people first." To find evidence that *yours* truly follows this philosophy, look to its decision-making. When your managers make decisions — big or small — what's their first criterion?

For the longest time, managers put process first. Organizations had processes, procedures, and policies for everything. They prized standardization, including of people (hence referring to them as "resources" and treating them as such).

Putting people first means starting decision-making with consideration of the people affecting it or being affected by it: the team, managers, users, buyers, etc. This is particularly significant in decisions that affect the system and people's experience inside it. The minimum standard for a people-first environment is for leaders to:

- Provide transparency — easy access to the information that guides decisions and actions.

- Make the work and its environment as motivating as possible, instead of relying on incentives to get people to do it well (or at all).

- Make boundaries explicit and expansive, and treat people fairly if they overstep them accidentally.

- Help people learn, grow, and take greater personal responsibility.

- Humanize staff, customers, and users — respect that they have whole lives, hopes and wishes, problems and needs, rationality and irrationality — and serve them accordingly.

At higher fitness levels, leaders do more and more of the following:

- Provide psychological safety: enable people to engage without fear of harm or retribution, and to do their work without fear of failure.

- Extend trust: assume that folks will act professionally and in good faith.

- Empower workers to make many of the decisions they're closest to, including decisions about their process. There might be a hierarchy, but it's rarely used for controlling people.

- Encourage collaboration where it matters, and make it possible.

Valuing people over process can yield superior fitness and results, especially as innovation and human ingenuity become ever more critical for competitive advantage. However, this value may be hard to defend and establish in a world of work that is used to valuing standardization. While standardization simplifies management and facilitates progress, it's sometimes applied too widely, as in the following examples:

- to people: "Resources" are put in teams based on their skills and availability and not on their interpersonal fit or synergy with teammates; they undergo the same performance evaluations as colleagues who do different work using a different way of working; policies are applied without allowance for context and nuance.

- to process: Projects with different needs are run with the same process, templates, and artifacts; so-called "best practices" are adopted even if they are not the best choice in the current context; recurring meetings always proceed the same way even if it's not engaging.

Work environments that need to minimize variability or to maximize user safety should indeed rely on formal practices and standard operating procedures. In knowledge work, like technology development, too much standardization stifles the variability inherent to learning, innovation, and problem-solving. It also creates tension, because human workers need compelling reasons to follow a given process, or at least to have some say over how they get their work done.

One of the strategies for moving from Level 1 to 2 involves determining the system's values and beliefs. If your company is not already explicit and consistent about putting people or process first, now is a good time to have conversations about that.

The traditional approach to value delivery structures is as functional parts with hand-offs. That might make managing it simpler but not necessarily very effective. Once you start thinking of it as a system and start seeing the relationships, the virtuous and vicious cycles, and the nonlocal effect of almost every decision, it's impossible to "unsee" them anymore. To deliver better results, base your decisions on system thinking and on an intentional and explicit mindset, be in tune with the culture, and respect the critical role that people — more than process — play in its success.

Building on this foundation, the next chapter explains what you need to know and do to lead fitness improvements in your system.

 SUPPLEMENTARY RESOURCE: Go to DeliverBetterResultsBook.com and download "Way of Working."

CHAPTER 3
LEADING FITNESS IMPROVEMENTS

Having read the first two chapters, you might be wondering: how can you possibly make all the changes this book suggests? From your position, you can control or influence only a part of value delivery.

That's a normal concern. If you're an engineering manager, you can influence only a team or two, and maybe not even all the members if the teams are cross-functional. If you're a product manager, you have little say over the developers' methods. If you're a project or program manager, you have accountability for an entire group's output, but you can't control everything about it. Even very senior people may not be in charge of an entire value delivery system.

In many companies, technological value delivery is made up of several separate functions, each with its own hierarchy. This structure will probably not go away anytime soon, and it doesn't need to. The various roles that take part in conceiving, making, and delivering technological products and solutions do different work, and there's value in specialization. Companies face challenges in improving value delivery because though the functions are interrelated, they tend to focus on their own parts.

And so, while this book addresses *you*, the reader, it is meant to be read by the many people, yourself included, who want or need to deliver better results and *share responsibility* for achieving that. Although improving the system ought to be a never-ending concern and commitment of top management, the responsibility isn't theirs alone. Other people who share it may be your colleagues in the same function, counterparts in another function, and managers above or below you. Some may be informal leaders. All of you, together, are the **improvement leaders**. Invite them to read this book so you all work with the same mental model. And then, facilitate powerful conversations and catalyze collective action using the questions in Appendix A.

Even though each one of you might have accountability for just a part of the system, you must all *make choices with the system in mind*. Build trusting relationships with each other, and act as *partners* — as opposed to one side leading an initiative and trying to get the others' buy-in or acquiescence. And when upgrading the system feels unglamorous and thankless compared to working on its product or solution, lean on your improvement peers as your support network.

> In early 2020, a company lost half of its Engineering staff and almost all of Product and Design. In May, it hired an experienced VP Engineering, who built up empowered teams and established a strong engineering culture. A few months later, the company brought in a new VP Product. From day one, the VP Engineering invited his counterpart to participate in *all* main decisions, and the VP Product did the same. They practically "traveled together" everywhere. A few months later, when they invited me to assess things and suggest further actions, I noted how integrated everything was. The two VPs had each other's trust to make decisions on behalf of the entire system, with the understanding that they wouldn't do anything to surprise each other.

This chapter describes the necessary foundation for leading fitness improvements in a system.

LEADERSHIP

If your actions or decisions regularly affect other people's experiences, choices, behaviors, and outcomes, you're leading them. It doesn't matter whether you are supposed to lead them, want to do that, or achieve favorable results. Your system has many leaders, each of whom affects the system's outcomes.

As a coach/consultant/trainer, I visit many work environments every year. In some, the leaders are busy planning and managing activities; they focus more on the work and less on how the human collective carries it out. In others, the vibe is different: their leaders also spend their energy and attention deliberately cultivating a particular culture that they believe will make their company successful. And if they haven't yet found the best culture for the company's mission, they keep at it; they upgrade both mindset and tactics, all the time.

What do you need for leading a value delivery system toward great fitness and results? Skills, models, tools, habits, and other people's support are important, but not as important as this key: *intention*. Be intentional about what you want the system *to be like* and the *choices* you want its people to make as they work toward objectives and outcomes. In your interactions, be clear and consistent about those choices, and always go back to why those specific ones were identified as most likely to bring success (more on this in Strategy 1b in Chapter 5).

Remember, too, that people respond to the environment they're in, and leaders affect the environment. Staff members won't work differently if management conducts business as usual. If delivering better results requires teams to work with a different mindset, such as adaptability over predictability and collaboration over siloed work, management needs to adopt and exhibit it before expecting the teams to do so. Otherwise, expect to see mistrust, cynicism, and disengagement.

Defining success

One thing you do as a leader is define success. Traditionally, that was easy to do: workers were successful if they finished tasks on time, and managers were successful if they hit their objectives or quotas. Fitness for purpose in today's world calls for defining success more richly, using outcome terms, and from a system perspective. For example, you might take the following into account:

- Two managers, who report to the same director/VP and whose teams have the same rate of delivery, may not be equally successful if one's teams are long-lived and the other's teams keep turning over and losing organizational knowledge.

- A team leader may make a much greater difference by being team "glue" and catching dropped balls than by writing a few more lines of code.

- Innovation work has a different success/failure profile than the implementation of a feature backlog.

Difficult work

Most likely, you and your company are good at doing hard work. How good are you at *difficult* work?[1]

You encounter hard work all the time in execution: managing backlogs, implementing features, deploying applications.

Difficult work requires you to make impactful decisions without a script. There's no shortage of it in value delivery: innovation, revising strategies and roadmaps, acting on negative feedback, saying "not yet" to stakeholders, learning fast and allowing failures, adjusting processes, and more.

Value delivery systems that have high fitness for purpose deal well with difficult work. Many of the recommendations in this book will help set your system up so it's possible, desirable, and safe to do the difficult work. Be prepared: implementing the recommendations is also difficult work.

Servant leadership and Agile leadership

The word leadership has always had different semantics than management, although to this day many organizations continue to use the two interchangeably. The fundamental distinction is that you *manage things* but you *lead people*. Even so, leadership has many forms and flavors; let's explore two that are getting more and more ubiquitous in various business contexts, and are very effective in enabling high fitness.

The first is servant leadership, which has leaders focus on maximally enabling their people — rather than directing them — to do their work in service of the mission and goals. This concept, first named in 1970, is based on the realization that it's complex human beings (not simple "resources") who produce business results. More specifically, several beliefs lie at the heart of servant leadership:

- People's engagement is voluntary, and they need some autonomy.
- People need their work to have a personally meaningful purpose.
- People take better action on ideas of their own.
- The people closest to the work should make most of the decisions.

Servant leaders shape their system to operate by these beliefs. They lead with purpose, empathy, and a positive attitude. They use influence and persuasion — rather than power and authority — with the people who work in it. As a result of all this, those people can do their best work *and* contribute to the system's fitness. This thinking is meant to be pragmatic, not touchy-feely.

I work with many managers who find this idea compelling yet challenging to implement. It runs counter to a traditional management ethos, which still exists in their companies to a large extent. That ethos also perpetuates itself: through structure (top-down), style (command and control), role descriptions and expectations (accountabilities), rewards (promotions and bonuses), and language ("drive results"). Meanwhile, servant leadership — though already a 50+ year-old concept — seems like a gamble and its name has unhelpful connotations. Even if the managers would ideally like to relinquish control, they're afraid to, especially if they don't fully trust their staff to deliver the correct results. And, since their small teams can know and do only so much within the bigger context, they struggle to balance control and autonomy.

Despite these challenges, more and more leaders have been applying servant leadership tenets in their organizations and demonstrating their effect on company results. In fact, as you'll see later in the book, achieving high fitness levels requires greater worker participation and ownership, which are enabled by servant leadership.

The other form of leadership is the Agile one. With Agile's rising popularity in the early 2000's, it became clear that servant leadership was necessary for real agility. However, while organizations have indeed been allowing teams greater control of their work, many have landed on unhealthy and ineffectual leadership patterns such as these:

- Team-level leaders, such as Scrum Masters, employ Agile leadership principles in their bubble. Meanwhile, the more-powerful organization around them does not.

- Managers allow folks to choose their tasks from a sprint backlog, but don't empower them further.

- Senior managers think they serve their teams when they say, "I don't care how you execute as long as you deliver on the plan," which ignores the realities of Agile work.

If your system's target operational model is based on the Agile mindset, avoid or overcome these patterns by adopting a richer view of Agile leadership, one that supplements the servant leadership model with these beliefs:

- People need to feel enough psychological safety before they'll bring their best selves to work.

- To best help the company achieve its mission, teams should have a high level of autonomy.
- Self-direction does not imply smooth flow.
- Teams may need help evolving to greatness.
- Upgrading the system's way of working will be more effective than dealing with each team or function individually.

Put another way: don't think about Agile leadership as merely marshaling a cross-functional team of professionals working in short cycles. Think of it as enabling an entire complex human system, operating according to Agile principles and values, inside a bigger complex context. This expanded perspective reframes team-level leadership as facilitating real teamwork, among willing participants, connected to the larger dynamic and purpose. It focuses mid-level and senior leaders on enabling larger groups' culture and systems. All these leaders are definitely not servants, but bona-fide *leaders* who focus on others before themselves and serve the greater whole. Creating this kind of leadership will help your system achieve its fitness goals faster and sustain them better.

LOOKING AFTER THE WAY OF WORKING

In your system, multiple people *look after the work*: determining deliverables, prioritizing them, coordinating workers' activities, and so on. Ideally, some people *look after the way of working* — the mindset and tactics in use both at the strategic level and day-to-day.

Whether it's the same people or not, make sure this responsibility has a publicly recognized "home." That home is a certain set of improvement leaders (as defined at the beginning of this chapter) collaborating and laser-focused on improving the system's way of working. Without this leadership, the system's fitness may erode unnoticed;

changes to the way of working would be made only reactively, possibly by a busy executive who doesn't specialize enough in this matter to respond effectively.

> *"Some organizations prioritize only the end result, disregarding the valuable work that these managers do to ensure system functioning (sometimes even looking down on them as 'non-technical'). However, organizations that prioritize both the 'what' and the 'how' of their work are better equipped to achieve resilience and high performance."*
>
> — *Dinah Davis, former VP of R&D at Arctic Wolf Networks*

Be careful: don't parcel out the responsibility across parts of the system. For example, don't solve for development separately from UX and separately from product management, etc. As mentioned earlier, this approach — the default in most companies — is suboptimal. Remember that in a system, the interactions between parts may matter more than the parts themselves.

In some situations, this responsibility may belong to a single person with overarching authority, such as a VP of Technology. In other situations, it's in the hands of a full-time team such as R&D Operations. And in other cases, a team of leaders shoulders it in addition to their regular work.

The team approach emerged years ago as an effective pattern in companies transitioning to an Agile operating model as a way to increase fitness. Such a team often has two interlocking purposes: to guide coherent organizational Agile adoption, and to support teams' and management's growth in Agile. The name of this team varies: Agile Leadership Team (ALT), Transformation Team, Enablement Unit, Lean-Agile Centre of Excellence, etc.

Effective teams share several characteristics:

- They have a clear purpose, vision, strategy, and roadmap, all of which align to the company's.
- The team's leader has a seat at the management table.
- The members hail from different parts of the system, not only from IT/engineering.
- The members have diverse specialties and backgrounds, rather than being uniformly Scrum Masters, coaches, program managers, or directors.
- The team has a budget, its own reporting line, an executive sponsor, and the backing of several other executives. They can put several initiatives in motion with little friction.
- They are known around the company (or at least around the system) as the people to approach for support related to the way of working. They may build internal coaching and training capacity, or engage outside expertise, to provide that support.
- The members understand, and consistently communicate, that they're leading a holistic approach to working better rather than being a process or tool authority.
- Each member is there voluntarily, is personally invested in the team's mission, and can dedicate enough time and attention to it. If they have some other "day job," it doesn't get in the way.
- They partner with managers and executives on carrying out changes related to the way of working in their respective areas.

"Such a team needs to build awareness and desirability and to 'sell' the narrative. The team must include a senior leader who really wants to see

change in the way of working, thought leaders who
can activate it, and people who can lead change."

— *Dann Wilson, AVP, Global Agile Office, Manulife*

This kind of team is often small, so it liaises with advocates (also called ambassadors) around the organization. These advocates help advance changes at the team level, and report back on needs, problems, and sentiments. While advocates may be managers, in many cases they are informal leaders — people with presence, communication skills, credibility, or likability that makes people follow them.

There are other patterns for taking responsibility for improving value delivery, and the responsible entity might change over time.

> At the Digital Products department of a media corporation, the management team took charge of the way of working. When I started coaching them, the team numbered eight managers and directors, and their department was 100-people strong. Two years later, the team grew to 15 as the department swelled to 180 people. At that point, some improvement strategies were taken on by subteams; for instance, to reduce the technical cost of change (a Level 4 strategy), a Technical Agility Working Group came together, comprising three managers, one senior tester-programmer, and several advocates.

HELPING PEOPLE WITH CHANGE

Part of the reason organizational change is assumed to be hard, and change management receives so much ink in the literature, is that it involves complex human beings. Humans are neither programmable, controllable "resources" nor do they always act rationally and predictably. This fact has the greatest impact on how you support improvements to value delivery, because in applying the book's strategies, you'll interact with many people across multiple boundaries.

For these folks, working in your company is far more than an exchange of pay for labor; it has many facets, benefits, and effects. Every action that's meant to improve the system — not only this book's strategies, even innocuous-looking tweaks to procedures — will change their experience. When you and your fellow improvement leaders plan and execute changes, use the following guidance to make them more welcome and effective.

Presume there's fear. In organizations, fear is every-where, among both managers and workers. People fear harm to their livelihood, lifestyle, and relationships. They won't admit to the fear, but it comes through in their behaviors: placating, controlling, following orders, acting defensively, sticking to their job description, distorting or hiding information, etc. As you work with people — of all ranks — always presume they're experiencing some fear, and choose your actions and words accordingly.

Preserve identity and self-worth. For better or worse, most people see themselves through the lenses of their career progression, professional role, span of control, and accomplishments. Therefore, they also fear for their identity, status, and self-worth. Whether there are real threats or not, people act on the threat stories they tell themselves. Help them change their narrative while continuing to feel that they matter and are successful.

Amplify the sense of belonging. Humans are tribal, though how they define their tribes is somewhat loose. While companies try to anchor belonging to the shared mission and culture, it's my observation that often, people's belonging is more tied to how well work fulfills other needs. (I know many people who have stayed at their company only because they enjoy the relationships with their colleagues.) Nowadays, belonging is more complex and tenuous, due to the move away from offices and the greater diversity (such as generational and cultural) in teams. As you consider changes, assess their impact on people's sense of belonging. Where possible, create situations and conditions that amplify it; this is especially important if and when you restructure teams.

Consider the environment's effect on behaviors. Improving value delivery requires that people change their choices, actions, behaviors, and habits. In your career, you've probably seen several common approaches for inducing such changes: making rules and procedures; giving feedback; encouraging, threatening, or pleading; appealing to logic or self-interest; and providing rewards for the new behaviors. You've probably also seen that these options don't always result in actual change.

A key reason for that is that people's behavior is heavily influenced by the various environments or systems they inhabit, such as their team, company, social circles, and family. Each environment has narratives and norms, considers some things more important than others, rewards certain actions and punishes others, sets expectations and exerts pressures, divides resources with some unfairness, and is a source of belonging and self-worth.

For instance, there's more to work in your company than the mission, product/solution, reporting structure, and ways of working. Other behavior-affecting elements of it include competition for bonuses, promotions, and recognition; the risk of being laid off; what some people owe to others; the trust between people and their managers; and opportunities for growth. And that's just the environment you lead in. Your followers inhabit other environments that are entirely outside your reach.

W. Edwards Deming famously said, "A bad system will beat a good person every time."[2] When you're trying to influence a change in people's behavior, consider first: What part of the current behavior is due to the environment they're in, and why is it like that? And then consider: What needs to be different about it to give rise to the preferred behaviors?

Avoid measuring individual performance. A staple of traditional management is to measure and manage the performance of individuals, with the aim being to improve the performance of the overall team/department. However, if you agree that value delivery is a dynamic process that occurs within a system, then you'll see that a person's performance doesn't fully arise from their choices, and that individuals' performance doesn't roll up neatly to that of the system. Moreover, when people know that they're being measured and the numbers have consequence, they'll modify their behaviors to make the numbers come out good, potentially at the expense of other desired outcomes (back in school, if you ever studied just enough to pass a test and, after it was over, forgot what you learned, you'd know this phenomenon). Certainly help folks with feedback during change, but manage and measure performance at the system level, not the individual one.

Be judicious about incentives. People respond to incentives, but not always in the way you hope or expect them to. Some extrinsic motivators, such as praise and money-equivalent rewards, can influence short-term changes but compromise long-term motivation. Replace these with acknowledgement and recognition to fuel folks' sense that they and their contributions matter. In parallel, create conditions that fulfill their needs for autonomy, mastery, purpose, enjoyability, and challenge (all of which vary from person to person and across situations). That's how you'll help sustain motivation — and thereby make fitness for purpose possible — for the long term.[3]

Put in new habits. Habits are subconscious patterns of behavior. They help us perform complex tasks, thereby taking some load off our limited-bandwidth, power-hungry conscious minds and helping us get more easily through life. For this reason, most of the actions and behaviors you see at work are habitual, not deliberate. Since the subconscious mind sees habits as beneficial, it resists changing them. As you notice elements of the current way of working that require changing, understand which ones are habitual; rather than try to get rid of them, try introducing new habits and gradually reinforcing them to displace the old ones. If you introduce completely new elements to the way of working, look for opportunities to make them habitual (this is a basic idea in Scrum, for example: run recurring team touchpoints on a fixed cadence).

Receive permission to coach. A powerful enabling stance for supporting change is coaching. If you use it, be aware that coaching another person requires their *permission* — every time — even if they report to you and coaching is part of your job description. By granting you permission, they also demonstrate being open to your support for their growth and change.

Understand how humans experience change. Ever wonder why some changes take a really long time or fizzle out? The Satir Change Model[4] provides an important explanation. It predicts that after a change occurs, there's a *chaos* stage of underperformance and confusion. To emerge

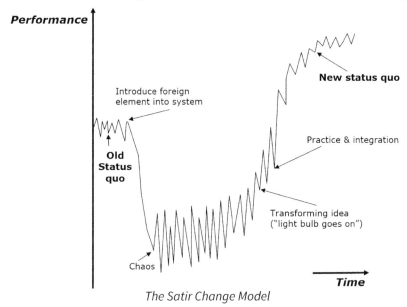

The Satir Change Model

from it, people need to have a *transforming idea*. Only then they can truly integrate the change for a new status quo. This pattern applies to big changes ("We're adopting continuous delivery!") and to small ones ("Let's run our daily Scrum differently."), both at work and in personal life.

The transforming idea is a fundamental shift for the person: they realize what the change really means, discover critical nuances, adjust their mindset, see the change from a different angle, overcome hangups, etc. It's critical for real change, but it's not guaranteed to occur, and it is impossible to know how much time will pass before it happens.

PROACTIVE BEHAVIORS FOR LEADING FITNESS IMPROVEMENTS

This book suggests ten specific strategies that you and fellow leaders can implement to deliver better results. To execute them more effectively and easily, make the following proactive *behaviors* habitual. Many of these behaviors will also make you a more effective leader in other contexts.

Lead with purpose

A staple of modern thinking comes with many names: lead with purpose, begin with the end in mind, and start with why. It usually applies to engaging individuals and teams. The idea of leading with a meaningful *why* instead of with the *what* or *how* has compelling benefits: people will do more of the right and less of the wrong; they'll be more motivated to act and take greater responsibility; they'll have more options for achieving the result, which can increase both effectiveness and efficiency; to the extent they make decisions, they can make better ones.

The same concept applies to making choices about the system's way of working. However, most people don't really pay attention to the way of working; it quickly becomes habitual, even if it's no longer a perfect fit. As tactical matters (process, practices, tools, and the like) come up in conversations, view them through the lens of purpose: how they help solve the right problems or achieve the right goals, and ultimately help the company achieve its mission and objectives.

Articulate assumptions

I regularly see leaders pondering questions such as these: "What product development capabilities will we need next year?" "What will make our users/customers leave us for the competition?" "Which technologies will we need to upgrade?" "What can we do to improve our KPIs?"

What I see less, however, is the leaders articulating the assumptions underlying their answers, discussing them with peers, and agreeing about validating some of them. What's worse, they don't design the way of working in light of that narrative or update it when the narrative changes. Instead, the way of working evolves as a patchwork of solutions to value delivery problems, folks work at cross-purposes, and the system's fitness for purpose sometimes even drops.

Keep on top of the assumptions that guide the system. Like purpose and values, make sure they are explicit, shared by all, and kept current.

Make boundaries clear

Every system has *boundaries* that separate it from other company systems. For instance, Product Development doesn't forecast next year's revenue, and HR doesn't write code. Most systems also have *internal* boundaries: which individual or group "owns" what.

Inside boundaries, people have room to decide and act. When they have greater *empowerment* or *autonomy*, they have more of that room. How much of it is helpful, and what it optimally looks like, are specific to each system and its fitness level. Some of the ten improvement strategies address that.

Whatever the boundaries are, make them clear and real. If people are aware of theirs (and believe they're real), they'll exercise their agency to that extent. If they don't know their boundaries, they'll operate with less agency than they actually have. They'll play it safe, not risking a stumble past an invisible line, and expect management to decide more and drive more. This shrinks the boundaries further, reducing the potential fitness.

Create psychological safety

In a given work context, folks need to feel *safe* enough to act despite fear and risks. If they don't feel safe enough, they behave in ways that limit fitness and that may impact their mental health. Safety progresses through the following four stages[5]:

- Feeling *inclusion safety*, people can be themselves as they participate in a group.

- With *learner safety*, they can ask questions, try things, and make some mistakes.

- With *contributor safety*, they participate in value creation as full members of the team, and can deliver bad news.

- Having *challenger safety*, they can question the status quo and offer improvements.

Creating safety takes intention, attention, and time; destroying it can be inadvertent and quick. Chapters 5-8 provide guidance on the type of safety to cultivate at each fitness level.

Build trust

Unlike safety, which is largely a matter of the system, trust is a personal matter dependent on both competence and character. Do you trust your colleagues or direct reports to perform their key duties well? Do they trust you to take their best interests into consideration? Do you trust your superiors and stakeholders to always make customer-friendly choices? Like safety, trust among people influences their behaviors;

low trust places a hidden "tax" on every interaction, making work harder and slower.[6] Conversely, when trust grows, people reach shared objectives more quickly and easily, and they feel safer, which increases the system's overall fitness. Help everyone around you recognize areas of low trust, extend trust to others, and adopt trust-building behaviors.

Invite and involve

Humans need to have a sense of control over what happens to them. The employees in your company are aware that it may dictate changes, but they also expect to have some agency when the changes affect how they work. As you implement the strategies, strike a careful balance; avoid situations like this one I heard from a product manager: "My company moved to [popular framework] about a year ago and the process being pushed down is overwhelming and burning everyone out." Don't mandate or dictate; instead, invite, involve, and lead with a compelling vision. Remember, the process should serve the people who use it, not the other way around.

The strategies also affect and involve various levels of management. The sense-of-control matter plays out differently there, because managers do have the power to control certain aspects of work so that workers produce desired results. Increasing system fitness requires changes to decision-making and ownership; it's only natural for a manager to feel a threatening loss of control, and to respond by interfering in the roles they have empowered to make decisions. Address this by having all managers participate in shaping these changes, so they continue to have their needs and objectives met in a healthy way.

Watch the work, not the workers

For your system to achieve its purpose, it needs to move correct work along. For that, it has mechanisms both for watching the work and for watching the workers.

Many companies are still used to *watching the workers* a lot. They do that by collecting timesheets and measuring individual productivity, by looking for unused time, by managing people's specific activities and task lists, and so on.

Watching the work, by contrast, includes monitoring each work item's progress through the pipeline (such as with a Kanban board), managing quality, coordinating integration, etc.

Some of the strategies for Level 2 and higher will guide you to build mechanisms and controls into the system so that the workers can watch more of the work, which frees up management to watch the system. In general, strive to reduce the watching of the workers because it signals mistrust and encourages behaviors that don't help fitness.

Help people behave congruently with the chosen mindset

The design of the system, such as its team structure, process, and practices, will change as its fitness increases. The key determiner of the design — the values — likely won't change. As explained in Chapter 2, the system's values express what its actors optimize for in order to be successful; for instance, in one system they might value "making a difference to users frequently" while in another it's "getting deliverables right the first time."

In one of the Level 1 strategies, you'll collaborate with senior leaders on determining that short list of values, articulating the beliefs that justify them, and choosing the operational principles that manifest them. That mindset — invisible and abstract — is fundamental to all subsequent investment in improving the system. As mentioned in Chapter 2, mindset matters more than tactics, and making only tactical modifications — to processes, tools, roles, and so on — is not enough to change it. Just as leaders ensure continued alignment to the company's mission and objectives, they should do so for the mindset too; otherwise, people will make contradictory choices when carrying out their work, which will diminish the results.

Help everyone update their mindset and adopt behaviors and habits that embody the chosen values and principles. Examples of such behaviors include explaining decisions, which demonstrates transparency; basing reactions to others on the assumption that they mean well, which manifests the principle of respect; and seizing opportunities to work together rather than pass work to others, which furthers collaboration. Model these behaviors yourself, consistently and authentically.

This is something you'll have to do all the time, because adopting new values isn't like throwing a switch. The people in the system may experience different journeys, and (being human) they will probably act inconsistently every now and then. You'll need to be patient, respectful, and consistent about reinforcing the target state, but also pragmatic.

Help people build self-sufficiency on the mindset and tactics front. Teach them the concepts and the options, so they get comfortable thinking about ways of working, but be careful of overwhelming them. Avoid spoon-feeding them answers; they shouldn't rely on you to determine which practices are right for them. For the best results long-term, act as partner, coach, or sounding board. When in doubt, opt for coaching and its key techniques: asking open questions, providing feedback, and waiting silently for the other person to think and speak.

In an example, suppose a team is adopting a flow model and needs a task board. If you design one for the team or provide them with a "standard" one, they might use it, but not learn how to make it fit their needs better. Instead, walk them through the principles and choices involved in designing useful boards, and support them as they create one.

As you apply this advice, you might experience a special kind of friction: certain company-level *business practices* limit your system's fitness potential and clash with some of your intended changes. Two common examples are annual budget cycles and individualized performance management along a curve; you might find other examples in hiring, contracting, and procurement. If you encounter such business practices, collaborate with the relevant leaders on adjusting them or making exceptions for your system. You have options; these days, there are new approaches for many such business practices, and although they're not yet as ubiquitous as some of the existing standards, enough companies have proven them out.

Be aware of your words

Humans can handle abstract concepts, but their words for concepts may not land with other people the way they intend. Examples of such words in a work context include: commitment, requirement, quality, consensus, efficiency, plan, estimate, accountability.

In some cases, people simply define those words differently. For example, many people interpret collaboration as "working together toward a shared result." To me, the standard's higher: "working together from a place of owning the result together." Or, if you ask someone, "Do you have a plan for X?", they might hear "Have you made a detailed list of activities?" while you meant "Do you know how you'd tackle this?" You can prevent misunderstandings by explaining what you mean by a certain term. This is especially important in three situations:

- when using terms that are often conflated with similar-sounding but different ones (such as effective/ efficient, accountability/responsibility, collaborate/ cooperate, accurate/precise, consensus/consent)
- when speaking with people who do different work but use the same terms
- when speaking with people whose native language is different than yours

The more challenging case is when terms are used that have unhelpful connotations and implications. For example:

- Some companies use the word "ticket" to denote the development team's unit of work. This word tends to focus attention on "what to do" and away from "why do it" (customer need, intended outcome, the meaning of the work). When a team's work is an endless stream of such to-do's, the effect on members is demotivating.

- Referring to team meetings as "ceremonies" sometimes leads people to think of them as boring process overhead, as opposed to opportunities for making important team decisions.

- Referring to people as "resources" equates them with the sum of their technical skills. It reflects a worldview that ignores many of the human matters mentioned in the previous section. Without explicitly respecting the full humanity of so-called "resources," attempts at creating psychological safety, ownership, and teamwork will come off as disingenuous or hypocritical.

A person's words reflect their model of the world. Get in the habit of noticing how others interpret your words, and encourage fellow leaders to notice whether the terms they use help or hinder what they're trying to accomplish and what they want to be like.

Beware over-simplification

People (and entire organizations) naturally want the best results, for minimum effort, every time. To achieve that, they pursue simplifications such as artifact standardization, task specialization, process automation, and blessed-by-others "best practices." These simplifications are great in some contexts and poor in others; they also sometimes blind people to additional options. To improve fitness for purpose, notice when people consider choices that appear too simple for the situation. Help them to understand the pros and cons and to consider more flexible, customized, and nuanced alternatives.

Trade rules for guidelines, agreements, and norms

Every organization, wanting to ensure correct and efficient execution, relies on rules to make certain aspects of the way of working explicit, uniform, and predictable. Common examples include templates for capturing backlog items and the need to get a manager's approval for every expense.

While human beings need rules to maintain societies and operate businesses, they don't always like having them. In team-based product development, people want to exercise some freedom and judgment, which is all the more necessary when they work on a problem they haven't solved before.

Assuming the system adheres to explicit values and principles (as recommended here), minimize your use of rules, and as fitness increases, relax the ones you keep. As a first step, trade your rules for guidelines. Try to go further and replace them with explicit agreements. Ideally, rely on norms and expectations. Do this carefully; the more you "loosen" rules, the more shared understanding and trust the group needs.

Help build cross-functional relationships

It takes a large and diverse group to deliver value to customers. The work is hard enough that people naturally focus on their own work and interact primarily with those they identify as their team. Help them expand their circle of engagement:

- Widen the definition of team (think "product community").
- Encourage people to form networks across silos.
- Create opportunities to connect, and reduce barriers to doing so.

The greater sense of belonging, and the clearer view of the big picture, will translate to higher-quality results.

Chris Mause, VP of Technology, Apriva:

"When a new VP of Sales joined the company, the president and I told her, 'You are going to be invited to a whole bunch of sprint reviews. This is how we do things around here.' Her department, in turn, started conducting bi-weekly 30-minute 'Top Opportunity Reviews' with the whole company.

My department liked knowing why they were working on certain features. When priorities changed, teams no longer groaned. When the sales people talked about risks with certain opportunities, the developers often came up with ways to help address those risks. The biggest thing this approach has changed was the tension between sales and development. We all celebrate closing deals, and when deals fall through, we all share in the loss."

Support people differently along the change curve

Each of the ten fitness-improving strategies in this book will affect people throughout the system. The Satir Change Model mentioned earlier posits that people experience every change as a sequence of stages, all of which feel different and require different kinds of support.

The first stage after kicking off a strategy will be Chaos. In this stage, competent people — who have been following the current way of working — find themselves in unfamiliar territory. Those who struggle with it might reject it as a bad idea. If that coping strategy fails, their next natural reaction will be to think "What's wrong with me? Why am I not getting this?" Treat them gently and help them be kind to themselves: the rocky period is not a reflection on their abilities but on their being human.

Exhorting them to "give it time," "do their best," or "fake it till they make it" is not a winning strategy. Instead, figure out what type of fundamental shift (the Transforming Idea, as explained earlier) can help. Make it more likely for them to reach that stage by empathetically providing feedback, opportunities for reflection, and space to try things out safely. You'll want people to reach that stage quickly, but not only because that's good for business. The longer people spend in Chaos, the likelier they are to experience failures and setbacks that may make them give up. Unfortunately, getting the Transforming Idea is not a matter of serendipity or elapsed time. Make learning, at this point in time, at least as important as delivering results.

The next stage, called Practice and Integration, will take a different amount of time depending on the strategy. At this stage, folks understand the updated way of working and feel okay with it, but don't yet necessarily perform it well. Make sure they have enough bandwidth and attention to practice it so it becomes habitual and unlikely to revert.

Be committed but not attached

A leadership stance I've found particularly powerful is "committed but not attached": be committed to a valuable outcome, but not attached to a particular way of achieving it. For example:

- Be committed to helping people work, review, and adapt in short cycles, but not attached to those cycles always being two-week long sprints. Depending on the situation, different cadences and planning approaches may be more useful.

- Be committed to people's growth and self-sufficiency, but not attached to achieving that primarily with coaching. Pick a helping stance based on the person and the situation.

- Be committed to creating environments that enable the growth of strong and productive teams, but not attached to having all members sit together in the office all day, every day.

This stance is closely related to leading with purpose and to autonomy. It facilitates coming up with options that may increase fitness. It also increases people's trust and belief in you, which will make it easier to lead further improvements.

 SUPPLEMENTARY RESOURCE: Download the "Proactive Behaviors for Leading Fitness Improvements" handy summary from the book's companion website, DeliverBetterResultsBook.com.

Improving a system's fitness for purpose is a deliberate, collective, continuous effort. It takes leadership that's attentive to ways of working, to the humans who use them, and to those humans' experience of change. Leaders must be aware that even when not actively focusing on improving fitness, their behaviors affect it; by making certain behaviors habitual, they maximize the chance of achieving favorable outcomes.

With clarity of the necessary foundation for leading fitness improvements, you can now proceed to learning about the specific strategies for each level. Before doing so, be sure to read Chapter 4 for a pathway to executing them.

CHAPTER 4

EXECUTING THE IMPROVEMENT STRATEGIES

In the previous chapter, we looked at leading fitness improvements in general. In this chapter, we focus on preparing for and executing the ten specific strategies described in the remainder of the book.

READY, WILLING, AND ABLE

As you and your fellow improvement leaders kick off any of those strategies, the affected people — both staff and management — need to be ready, willing, and able to apply it.

To be **willing**, people generally need you to provide more than a compelling vision or target state. They need to trust your intentions, to feel safe about the choices, and to feel that you care about them as individuals (not just about the company). These feelings will motivate them more than a logical list of the strategy's benefits. And, to make it less theoretical or daunting, *tell stories* of success that people can relate to.

A European designer and manufacturer of an important accessory started an Agile pilot project in R&D in 2022. It moved very slowly, because the team was only 10%(!) dedicated to it.

There was another slow-moving project in the pipeline. One day, the CEO happened to see a prototype. Excited, he gave an R&D manager three months to finish that part, which would normally take 18. Going against the company's strategy of running dozens of projects in parallel, he effectively said, "On this one, we value having a customer-ready product soon." The manager had to work very differently to accomplish that.

He assembled a cross-functional team, and within one month, they made a year's worth of progress. How? With a barebones process based on three basic Agile/Lean principles: eliminating delays and waiting periods, collaborating instead of handing off artifacts, and always making small meaningful progress.

Afterwards, the manager convened his counterparts and told them the story, leading up to two main lessons. One: see what we can accomplish when we optimize our way of working for different effects. Two: it's possible here! His peers were excited, and planned to apply these ideas to all R&D projects in 2023-24.

Two enemies of willingness are inertia and inattention, and they feed each other. Every company has plenty of work to keep itself busy, such as customer commitments, product enhancements, and keeping the lights on. So much so, that there's never a good time to try process improvements or to take training. You can easily detect this inertia in your system: just observe how long people can pause from their "productive" work before they (or their managers) get nervous about meeting obligations. In turn, the unrelenting focus on plans, tasks, and deliverables often draws attention away from how the system operates. When that does become an object of attention, a fear of jeopardizing commitments keeps the system from changing.

When building up willingness, be careful about how you speak about the current state. Talk about the problems that the customers, the company, and your own people experience, while also highlighting the positives. Avoid value judgments saying the system's broken, dysfunctional, outdated, or wrong — and don't blame past leaders and decisions either. Remember: people are doing what they can with the resources they have in the environment they're in, and such statements will only make them defensive. Be extra judicious when speaking with middle and senior managers who have grown in the system, playing by its rules; their experience in it is linked to their self-worth.

> If your target model is based on Scrum, you might have heard the expression "Scrum exposes dysfunction." The idea is that if you're struggling to implement it effectively, this is indicative of dysfunction. This is both false and unhelpful. What adopting Scrum does expose is a gap between the current set of values and the desired one; that gap is legitimate if the system is still transitioning between them. Save the word "dysfunction" for where it applies: The system's approach and methods can't possibly yield hoped-for results, or it is in denial of its de-facto value set.

To be **able** to carry out the change, people need to understand it and its implications. As needed, provide training to develop the relevant mindset, capabilities, and skills. If the needs of leaders and individual contributors overlap substantially but not fully, consider providing separate training opportunities: some that they can attend together and thus increase the feeling that they're in it together, and some that cover particular needs. Use simulations and games — not slide presentations — to get key points across. Conduct "dry runs" with real examples to understand gaps. When folks feel more *able* to work differently, they'll be more likely to be *willing* to.

To be **ready**, the timing needs to be good. Times of unusually high pressure are often not great for making changes, because people focus on the work, not on how they do it. Having said that, if unrelenting pressure is the norm, your system's performance will never improve, and may even decline if left unchecked. Find the time, even if it means starting small, so you can balance managing the present with preparing for the future.

Fortunately, most strategies integrate easily with everyday work (for example, stabilizing the system in Level 2, or increasing safety, teamwork, and collaboration in Level 3). Others need concentrated action. However, none of them require pausing work.

Remember from Chapter 3 that people have limited mental and emotional capacity for change, especially for the ups and downs of the Chaos period *and* while still having to get their work done. Additionally, for each strategy to stick, they need to experience the Transforming Idea and go through enough of the Practice and Integration stage. That's why most strategies take months to become habitual. Leadership must allow enough bandwidth and focus and be *patient* — not to take premature corrective action if the transforming idea doesn't appear quickly.

A PATHWAY FOR EACH STRATEGY

It bears repeating that all ten strategies need to be applied holistically — throughout the system, not in parts. For example, at Level 2, stabilizing the system means more than just smoothing out cycle times in development; it means creating balance between supply and demand all the way from idea to delivery.

This might sound daunting, but it's not all on you. In addition to working with the other improvement leaders and getting the backing of your superiors, you'll likely partner with various managers on carrying each strategy out. You're probably already used to partnering cross-functionally on moving work along, such as when solving certain problems or coordinating delivery. Although partnering on *how* they and their people work might be an unfamiliar experience, it's entirely practical if you build trusting relationships with them. Share the book's lessons with them, or invite them to read it (at least Chapter 1), so they understand where you're coming from.

Minimize reliance on formal power (positional authority) and prefer influence instead. Everyone will be more likely to go along with the changes in the presence of respect, psychological safety, trust, and transparency. If influence doesn't work, your fallback is negotiation and compromise. You might need to work around some people.

Senior leaders and stakeholders may be sponsors or allies for the effort. When you interact with them, you'll gain more support by spending as little time as possible on the tactical side of changes, and instead connecting the changes to business effects. Such effects include better customer outcomes, lower risk, fewer lost opportunities, and reduced unnecessary work (which would free up funds for investment in other potentially winning ideas). If necessary, help them expand their view of the technology part of the company beyond the construction of software.

If you're worried that a strategy might sound alien, feel overwhelming, or be unwelcome, look for precedents of partial application. For example:

- Strategy 1a (manage the project portfolio): There must have been a time when a team of senior managers had to aggressively prioritize projects and initiatives, going as far as parking some of them. How did that come about? How did it positively affect the work that did get prioritized, the system, and the entire company?

- Strategy 1b (design the way of working): Has the company ever needed to run a certain project differently from the norm? Why was that? How was the special process determined, and what were the results?

- Strategy 3b (defer commitments and increase release frequency): Has there been a successful project that progressed with relatively few commitments and constraints? Can that explain some of its success or certain positive dynamics that occurred during execution?

Plenty of empirical evidence shows that mandating a change in the way of working is a non-starter, as well as a violation of the "putting people first" value. Also out is telling people the change is optional and then proceeding to cajole, exhort, pressure, lecture, incentivize, or encourage them to say yes. Instead, follow this pathway — which addresses the ready, willing, and able preconditions — with each strategy:

1. Articulate the reasons for making changes now.

Speaking only with the other improvement leaders at this point, achieve clarity and alignment on the motivation for improving value delivery *specifically now*. What problems will that address? Is there a specific urgency or opportunity? Why not wait? You should all bring up your concerns and reckon with them now, before you commit publicly to making a system-wide change.

2. Get full clarity on the system's current workings.

Still working only with your fellow improvement leaders, develop a clear picture of how the system works *now* in the context of the strategy. Understand the interactions between its parts, the forces and influences, the mindset that guides people, the constraints, the virtuous and vicious cycles (loops), and so on.

For example, doing that for Strategy 3b (defer commitments and increase release frequency) might include the following steps: Study what commitments are made, by whom, and how. Map out the effects they have on various parts of the system and elsewhere in the company. If the commitments are far-reaching or very specific, seek to understand why. Get data on release frequency and learn who determines their content. Discover the effects of the release frequency on people's behaviors.

This is an important activity that doesn't need to take long. Done well, it reveals risks and barriers as well as intervention points, so you can implement and execute the strategy effectively.

3. Help people understand the strategy.

Explain the strategy to the people it affects. Don't assume that some changes to process and structure are self-evident or common sense, because what's sensible is colored by one's mindset. When I help my clients with this step, I make the following assumptions:

- Most team members and managers haven't had opportunities to build a solid theoretical foundation for process decisions.

- In part, that's because they're much more interested in their work than in its process.

- At the same time, they don't like to be told how to work.

Be genuine, transparent, and respectful. Seek to understand folks' concerns, and use that understanding to inform your next actions. If you encounter friction or negativity, remember that a lot of it is not personal but rather an effect of the system.

A stance I've found extremely useful for leading change-making is to be *curious, present, and empathetic* in conversations about the change.[1] Be curious about how the other person sees things; give them 100% of your attention; and be empathetic towards them. You'll defuse resistance, reduce misunderstandings, and build a relationship — all at once.

You might need to invest a little time and money on training to enhance knowledge, align assumptions, and allay concerns. If a change in mindset is required, the training should help folks understand how it differs from the mindset they hold currently (whether intentionally or unawares). Be wary of training that focuses on specific process frameworks or prepackaged practices, as it may not lead people to upgrade their *thinking*, and may leave them feeling stuck with a solution that isn't quite right for them.

4. Visualize the target state.

You've assessed the current state and learned about people's concerns and ideas. Now, collaborate on sketching a picture of a realistic and relevant target state: what might the system be like once the strategy has been executed long enough to be effective and sustainable? For example, if you're looking at Strategy 1a (manage the project portfolio), what might doing that regularly and reliably look like in terms of decision-making processes and touchpoints, and how will that affect the rest of the system? Or, if you're looking at Strategy 3a (increase safety, teamwork, and collaboration), what forms could effective inter-team collaboration take, and what processes and dynamics might change as a result?

Of course, you don't have a crystal ball, and you can't imagine or consider all possible scenarios. While each strategy has patterns, generally helpful techniques, and examples of successful implementations, each application of it is unique. There can't be a universally effective recipe, playbook, or set of "best practices" for it; real life is just too complex, and your context matters. Be committed to implementing the strategy, not attached to the exact eventual form of the way of working.

5. Plan the approach to the change.

Each strategy takes minutes to describe and months to make the change real and habitual. How will you approach its application: will you use predictive techniques and "roll out" changes, gradually or all-in? Will you start with an experiment, and then decide? How will staff be involved in decisions about the changes?

The answer, of course, depends on the situation; you might even approach each strategy differently. Nevertheless, chances are your situation is complex enough to benefit from a gradual, evolutionary approach, in which you arrive at the assumed target state via a few milestones of smaller changes. It's easier to gain support for such changes, and the frequent opportunities to reflect on progress enable course adjustments. For example, at Level 1, starting the portfolio-management strategy by only deferring a few portfolio items may improve the delivery of in-process items enough to generate support for full execution of the strategy.

If you follow a gradual approach, take the following two matters into consideration:

First, each of those smaller changes should make a meaningful and noticeable difference in the way of working. For example, when stabilizing a system (Strategy 2b) that has a high amount of unplanned work, halving it can make for a meaningful milestone.

Second, consider making the first small change or two a *safe experiment*: easy to undo with no repercussions. For instance, when designing the way of working (Strategy 1b), hold off on changing titles, reporting lines, or compensation until the system reaches a sustainable better state. Furthermore, if you'd like to emphasize the people-first value, invite staff to cocreate each experiment and subsequently to participate in learning from it. (If doing this feels inefficient and not a good use of staff's time, weigh it against the risk of low buy-in and wrong decisions.)

Naturally, your experience from working in other organizations will inform your choices here. Remember, though, that every context is unique. Different people work in your system. They are subject to different pressures and constraints. They have their own specific need for time, support, and adjustments to reach the destination.

In considering your approach, also decide whether you'll be self-sufficient or get some external support. While you personally might be used to the ideas in the strategies, it's safe to assume that most people experiencing the change are not; it's not their expertise or something they encounter frequently enough. Appropriate external support — mentoring, training, coaching — can reduce the risk and shorten the time to real and sustainable improvement, while communicating to folks that the change is real and has leadership's backing.

6. Execute the strategy.

Now, you can start executing the strategy. At the end of each strategy's section in this book you'll find guidance on how to go about that and how you'll know it's "done its part" for leveling up the system's fitness.

Assume it would be months before reaching that state. You and your fellow improvement leaders need to be patient and to have people's backs. This is a time of learning and growth, not of performance management. Keep communicating across the system to sustain the energy and motivation needed for the change. Rely on frequent messaging, sharing results and success stories, to reinforce new habits. For best results, communication should originate from three levels — senior leadership, middle management, and teams — on their respective cadences.

As mentioned before, the strategies from lower fitness levels ought to be second nature by now, implemented in mindset, tactics, and behaviors. Keep executing them and don't let them slip. For example, managing an appropriate number of active and committed portfolio items isn't something you do at Level 1 and then forget about it; at higher levels, keep protecting the portfolio from extra projects sneaking in. Or, also at Level 1, you'd set up the teams based on what matters most for achieving the mission and objectives; at higher levels, you may iterate on team boundaries and responsibilities.

7. Reassess frequently.

Each level has two or three strategies for reaching the next level. Each one of those strategies needs to fulfill specific criteria, which are largely subjective and qualitative, for the system to level up. Every few weeks, review progress with your colleagues, keeping in mind that some changes require time to settle and possibly even more time before there's enough data to discern patterns. Consider using the fitness assessment questions from Chapter 1, looking for movement in the ratings of fitness aspects and in the calculated raw fitness score. If some element of a strategy isn't taking hold, look for reinforcing loops in the system that prevent it from changing.

Remember that the system doesn't exist in a vacuum and that it's made up of human beings. It may experience internal shifts irrespective of the strategies, and its aspects' optimums may shift due to business and technological changes. As a result, its fitness for purpose — which is a relative measure — may change over time. Repeating the fitness assessment every now and then will help you react to changes sooner.

For an example of a company using the strategies to move Product Development from Level 1 to 4 in only ten months, read Appendix B.

If you're interested in my mindset training for leaders and team members, see the options on my website, 3PVantage.com.

HOW TO CONTINUE READING THIS BOOK

The next chapter explains the strategies that will move your system from Level 1 to 2. Subsequent chapters do the same for the higher levels.

Although you could jump straight to the chapter that corresponds to your system's current level, I suggest you first read the chapters leading up to it. They provide a comprehensive view of the lower-level strategies that should already be in place. If you notice gaps, close them using those chapters' guidance before executing the current level's strategies.

You don't need to worry about higher-level strategies, because your system is not there yet. You read brief summaries of them in Chapter 1; however, you might still like to read their chapters now, to get a stronger sense of the journey and to know explicitly what you *don't* need to implement yet.

CHAPTER 5
PROGRESSING FROM LEVEL 1 TO 2

At Fitness Level 1, the system is unable to contribute adequately to achieving company objectives. Despite hard work and some successes, the system's output falls short of what the business needs, on multiple fronts.

Managers and stakeholders often think that the development teams are the cause: they don't deliver enough, don't work on the most important things, don't estimate reliably, don't meet their commitments, etc. Development leaders attempt to fix the problem by restructuring teams or by changing the teams' process, for example by adding procedures and policies, cutting meetings, and collecting status more often.

All too often, this response is neither accurate nor sufficient; rather, the system's way of working needs a rethink.

However, that's only part of the story. Another problem keeps the system's fitness at Level 1: too many big-ticket items (projects, initiatives, features, etc.) are in flight or planned to be. A CTO gave me an example of that recently: his engineering department of 33 people, organized in five teams, has 55 such items.

Whether the many items come from a committed roadmap, an annual plan, stakeholders' objectives, or new circumstances, all of them fight for attention. Trying to get the teams to complete as many of the important and urgent ones as possible, management scrambles to align priorities and coordinate work. As a result of the teams' frequent context-switching and suboptimal way of working, they finish only a few items in an acceptable fashion. Management leans on the teams, but the pressure doesn't make the system produce better results. Meanwhile, more demand for big-ticket work arrives, and the cycle continues.

Two strategies help to escape this trap and reach Level 2: managing the project portfolio more tightly and strategically, and designing the way of working for the system's needs. The former ensures that the system's capacity is used for the right things, and the latter directs people's efforts toward better delivery of those things. While you can start executing both strategies at the same time, dovetailing them might be more helpful: reducing the active portfolio to focus on the most useful work may inform a more accurate determination of the way of working.

STRATEGY 1A: MANAGE THE PROJECT PORTFOLIO

At a high level, your system delivers features, makes technical upgrades, conducts experiments, and performs other units of work that are big enough to make a demonstrable difference to the customers/users and to the company. The system might manage these units as projects or programs of various sizes, combine them into product releases or milestones, or perform them on their own. I'll refer to all these units of work as *portfolio items*, and to the collection of current and upcoming items by the common term *project portfolio* (acknowledging that they might not all be projects). Your company might be using one of two other common terms, "roadmap" and "pipeline," which are close enough to "portfolio" for the purpose of this strategy.

Note: If your company is large enough to have two or more value delivery systems, each would have its own portfolio, and the set of them would roll up to the enterprise one. The advice given here applies at both portfolio levels.

Like every system out there, yours has more work than it can handle. The following approaches to juggling a high number of portfolio items are common, but they compromise many (and sometimes all) aspects of the system's fitness for purpose:

- Increase the number of teams by making each one smaller, even to the point of having less than four people on some teams. While this approach results in more projects being active at the same time, the duration of each might be longer. This might cause managers and stakeholders to put pressure (perhaps subtly) on teams to finish sooner, which could lead them to take shortcuts and compromise quality. Team members would be unlikely to get help from their former colleagues, because they would also be underwater with their own projects.

- Keep the teams' composition, but assign different projects to different members. This could have an effect similar to the first option, with the extra frustration of folks who are officially teammates but don't have opportunities to benefit from it.

- Keep the teams' composition and change the focus of each one as necessary, usually when something is escalated or reprioritized. The effect: teams start many projects and multi-task a lot, but don't drive toward *finishing and delivering* anything in particular. This approach can also greatly increase their frustration and stress.

- Hire more people or contract some work out. If your system were a busy highway, this would be akin to widening it, which usually causes more drivers to start using it, which merely shifts the location and size of the traffic jams. Increasing the number of individual contributors allows more work into the pipeline, but it doesn't necessarily result in finishing proportionally more work or in increased efficiency.

Solve this problem more effectively and sustainably by closely managing the portfolio: control how many items, and which ones exactly, the system has going on and committed at any given time. As you'll see in the explanations below, this strategy runs deeper and wider than typical prioritization. In fact, it's so foundational that, without implementing it, the other nine strategies in this book will not be effective and your system's overall fitness won't increase much.

How many portfolio items get worked on

Does your system have an *explicit* limit on the number of portfolio items that can be in flight or committed? If not, it probably has an *implicit* limit, which is largely a function of headcount and item size. Take a moment to think what that number is currently.

Since the system is at Fitness Level 1, chances are that the number is too high. You'll need to reduce it, possibly by a lot.

Are you thinking, "But we need to do all the work that comes to us!"?

If that's in fact true, what can you do about it? The approaches listed above won't improve the situation. On the other hand, reducing the burden of active and committed work tends to allow better processes and habits to emerge. Already in the short term, having less work-in-process (WIP) can improve quality, thereby reducing rework and emergencies and improving outcomes. As the system's fitness grows, it will become more productive and capable of responding to higher demand. Another benefit of the WIP limit is that it forces leaders, who might otherwise rank many portfolio items as a #1 priority, to actually prioritize them.

What should your portfolio WIP limit be? If it's too low, some workers might not spend their time usefully; if it's too high, the system will experience the dynamics and consequences described above. Determining the ideal limit early on is very difficult; it's not simple math based on the number of people and teams. Rather, it's tied to the entire system's ability to reliably produce quality results (not only in development!). And *that* is a matter of the type and complexity of the work, the availability and distribution of expertise, the nature and magnitude of technical pain points, and much more. As you apply the next strategy in this chapter, you might restructure your teams, but even the optimal arrangement presents a practical limit on their capacity.

This all might make it sound as if there's a single WIP limit that applies to the entire portfolio. However, it's usually better to place a separate limit on each processing stage that portfolio items go through. For one reason, different people do a different kind of work at each stage. For another, portfolio items don't all undergo the same end-to-end processing. Some are abandoned after inception or discovery; some require several discovery cycles before development; many benefit from interleaving discovery and development; some will have evolutionary milestones. Managing stage-specific limits takes more effort than managing a single limit for the entire portfolio, but it can improve the flow of work.

What to include in the portfolio

The portfolio is the single master repository for *all* big work: current, committed, and optional (valuable work that the system might commit to later, but hasn't yet). Its contents thus reflect something vital for the company: the strategy for creating value. Keep and maintain the portfolio in a central artifact; every other artifact you use for planning, such as OKRs and backlogs, or for communication, such as roadmap presentations and progress reports, should be based on this "source of truth."

I sometimes visit organizations that do not maintain a single explicit artifact for the portfolio. Their staff is busy, but the work is managed tactically, information about it is scattered and hard to understand, and some of the work doesn't get planned properly. This results in considerable inefficiency. Moreover, it creates difficulties for executives and system

leaders, who need transparency into what's being created and the business case for it to make strategic decisions.

At the level of the portfolio, it's helpful to think about outcomes: problems to solve, opportunities to seize, needs to fulfill, or goals to meet. The portfolio would thus include intended **customer outcomes** and for some of them, the means to achieve those outcomes, such as product features and projects. However, that's not enough. It must also include **business outcomes** — outcomes that your company cares about — since they ultimately enable it to keep delivering customer outcomes. Many business outcomes arise from internal improvement work, such as technical debt repayment, development pipeline upgrades, platform enhancements, and development of tools and reports. Other business outcomes arise from "invisible" work such as maintenance and defect fixes.

By including both types of outcomes in the portfolio, the system can more easily give both of them the attention they deserve, even though the underlying work can be very different. That will likely require business, product, and development folks to communicate and collaborate better with each other. If your portfolio contained only product work, the other kind would likely fight a losing battle for attention, and the system's fitness would degrade over time.

What information should you include per portfolio item (or per project/program, if that's how you manage the items)? At a minimum, articulate its intended outcomes and why they matter. Better yet, add its intended users/customers, success criteria or key results, constraints, and critical assumptions. You might also capture key risks, information about affected and involved parties, and the assumed level of effort. This information constitutes a simple charter (also known as "one-pager" or "brief") for the item.

Framing the work this way — rather than by merely listing deliverables — will help you compare portfolio items rationally and prioritize them strategically. By focusing on an item's outcomes and business context, everybody in the system can understand why it's chosen and see themselves contributing to it. While working on a given item, teams and leaders have a shared and agreed-upon basis for making tradeoffs. In my experience, the charter is an extremely important artifact; the few hours it takes to produce — ideally done collaboratively — can prevent wasting hundreds of hours on wrong work. Just like the portfolio, each charter is a living document.

Managing the portfolio

Visualizing the portfolio — rendering its information in a rich visual form — is key to its successful management. Effective visualization makes it easy for managers to collaboratively make intelligent decisions about the work to be done, and the transparency increases trust all around.

While there is no single, ideal way to visualize a portfolio, some popular formats tend to work well. Yet even if you pick one, expect to iterate on its design until it becomes effective and efficient for your needs. You might like to use two zoom levels: one that shows the overall set of work and where each item stands (the level that executives might care about), and a closer look with more detail, including dependencies. Keeping parked or rejected items in a separate section of the portfolio may help emphasize the value of the items that do make it through the system.

> *"We called our portfolio-visualization artifact 'the staffing plan.' Each row represented a team, and the columns stood for sprints and months. Based on low-fidelity, high-level estimates, we'd draw rectangular blocks across rows and columns to show who would work on what when. The plan was in Miro, and each block was linked to a Jira epic that had all the details;*

it was easy to manage without creating duplication. I met with the director of Product Management every week or two to refresh it based on Engineering's progress and on updated business plans, and I reviewed it with my teams every week to show them where we were going."

— Jay Allison, Sr. Director, Software Engineering at Synapse Wireless

Whether you use a portfolio or a roadmap to capture all "big work," be judicious about attaching dates to items. That will increase the system's ability to focus on the most *impactful* work. If everything has a ship-by date, the system effectively subscribes to the value of "deliver on time" above all other values, a choice that may not align with the intended mindset (which you'll articulate as part of Strategy 1b). Some items naturally require a fixed delivery date; others incur a cost or drop in value as they're delayed past some date; still others can wait a while. Knowing which is which — understanding their "cost of delay" profile — will help you sequence the work and improve system responsiveness and effectiveness.

The system should have a strong process for deciding how and when items initially get into the portfolio and later move into discovery and development. This process's decision-making framework should factor in the items' charters, their cost of delay, and the flow capacity of the *entire* system. Without such a process, the system is guaranteed to experience unnecessary bottlenecks and tensions. In a typical example, valuable ideas sit upstream for months of unhurried planning; when they finally get into development, they immediately become urgent (and late), leading to rushed work, quality compromises, and unwanted rework (which subsequently causes problems for other portfolio items).

If senior managers in your system find it difficult to prioritize big work even once they have an informative and visualized portfolio, the following principles and techniques may help:

- Manage the portfolio as a cross-functional team. Remember, it represents the work of the entire system. Even though system parts (such as Design or DevOps) might visualize their portions using separate artifacts, these should roll up to the portfolio.

- Instead of showing the items in a list and tagging each item with high/medium/low priority, use the physical ordering of items to communicate rankings. If you've ever sorted a list using sticky notes, it's the same idea: no two can be in the same place at the same time.

- If the portfolio is very large, determine enough of the top priorities to get the system working productively for a few weeks. The rest can wait for a later meeting.

- Whenever people say "yes" to more work, remind them (nicely) what they're saying "no" to: other important work, overall timeliness, the teams' sanity, the product's quality, and the ability to pivot. If you need a gentler way to get this point across, ask what they're *trading off*.

Jay Allison, continuing his story:

"This is where our staffing plan really shone. In order to squeeze something in, we literally had to drag another block out of the way to make room for it. The impact of unplanned work was extremely clear."

Executing this strategy

If there's no portfolio artifact yet, help the relevant decision-makers — ideally working collaboratively — to put one together. Start by mapping the workflow: the high-level stages that portfolio items travel through, from idea to delivery. Create a single artifact and capture *all* current and committed "big work" in it, indicating where each item is in the workflow. That will be a quick win. Don't worry yet about its exact format, or the process for organizing it; you won't get either of them perfect the first time anyway. The resulting collection might turn out to be so much bigger than your colleagues assume, that you'll get their attention and willingness to start reducing it.

A client's first attempt at visualizing the full portfolio. The columns represent the stages, and the card colors represent the type of each item (core product, modules, reactive work, potential add-ons).

Now, start using it regularly. Your system already has meetings where discussions about the high-level work take place; encourage the participants to work off the portfolio (instead of separate lists) and to update it as they make decisions. If such meetings happen more than once a month, the use of the portfolio may quickly become habitual.

Once you have a useful-looking artifact that contains the work, represents its flow, and shows where every item is, start limiting the number of items in each major stage in the workflow. Some stages are likely to include more work right now than the intended limit. You might be able to pause or cancel some of it, but if not, at least don't allow new work in. This will help you reduce logjams and make the limit more real going forward.

As the weeks go by, keep paying attention to the stage limits and enforcing them if necessary. Limiting work intake may feel alien and counterintuitive, especially to people who believe that using all available time maximizes productivity. Within a few weeks, you'll see which limits are good and which limits need to be increased or decreased. The visualization method you choose should make seeing that easy (a column-based board, common in Kanban systems, tends to be helpful).

Remember that the portfolio is there to support making strategic decisions. If you suspect that decisions aren't great despite managers' reliance on the portfolio, examine the information captured there and how it's visualized. Ineffective portfolios tend to be too simplistic, not informative enough about each item, or not reflective of the system's full workload.

Doing all this takes ongoing effort and attention from busy leaders across the system. In many companies, that is the reason it falls by the wayside, and fitness for purpose never really rises sustainably past Level 1. Ironically, though, it's one of the leaders' most important responsibilities — not just to lead the making of stuff, but to decide which stuff to make and which not to make. Solid portfolio management is a necessary enabler of regularly delivering strategically important work.

At the same time, portfolio management requires real accountability from the decision-makers. That's because their choices, and how frequently they change, have a large effect on effort, focus, and complexity and therefore on company results. For this reason, executing the strategy often requires the backing of executives; it can be hard to say "no" or "not yet" to important work, especially when it's tied to managers' objectives.

All this assumes that the company is not expecting from the system something it can't possibly provide. For an oversimplified example, say the company's strategic objectives need the system to produce 50 must-have outcomes a year, but even with the best leadership, portfolio management, and way of working it can only produce 20. The system's not at fault, but it can't succeed. If such a gap exists and the strategic objectives can't be dialed down, you'll need to expand the system.

This strategy will have "done its part" to get your system to Level 2 when on a regular basis, the portfolio's most important items aren't unacceptably delayed by less-important ones.

STRATEGY 1B: DESIGN THE WAY OF WORKING

For the longest time, the world of software development managed work using plan-driven, predictive approaches such as Waterfall and classic project management. Processes were well-documented, ubiquitous, and assumed to be efficient; effectiveness was implied.

In the 80's, Lean ideas trickled into software development. In the 90's, Agile methods emerged, and a few of them got packaged as frameworks. Many organizations still use traditional ways; many others rely on Agile frameworks, with or without customization; some use Agile tactics, thinking of them as modern software development but not calling them Agile; a few develop their own methods; and others copy and paste those methods. There is a lot less uniformity, which is good (because every company's different), but the options can be overwhelming.

This mess meets value delivery fitness in two ways. First, many leaders reach for their favorite *methodologies* or *frameworks* and try to make them work in their context. Leading options, at the time of writing, include Scrum, SAFe, and continuous delivery. Second, professionals — whether managers or individual contributors — tend to reuse *tactics* that they've used in other contexts. Examples of such tactics include estimating using story points, having separate development and QA teams, and announcing decisions only once they're finalized in a silo.

In both cases, people want to succeed and they mean well. Their choices would work well under certain conditions, but some don't work so well in their current reality. As a result, the system is not as fit for purpose as it needs to be.

Just as leadership of people is most effective when it's situational, so it is for the way of working. Strategy 1b is to design the system's way of working based on what matters most for achieving the mission and objectives. The challenge is to do so without jumping straight to the favorite, familiar, or popular. Helping my clients do that, I've found it most useful to "follow the arrows" in the Way of Working diagram that you encountered in Chapter 2 (included here again for your convenience):

1. Determine the future-looking values and beliefs for the system ("the story we want to tell" from now on).

2. Choose operational principles that embody those values and beliefs.

3. Determine the tactics.

Note: In a given context, leaders might know intuitively that Scrum, for example, is a great fit, whereas in another context they'd pick a more flow-based approach. When they're correct, it may be an indication that they've subconsciously followed these three steps. Still, get that information out of their heads by explicitly performing these three steps in a collaborative workshop, which will maximize accuracy of choice and shared understanding. It will also make everyone more likely to buy in to the intended way of working, because they'll understand why it looks the way it does.

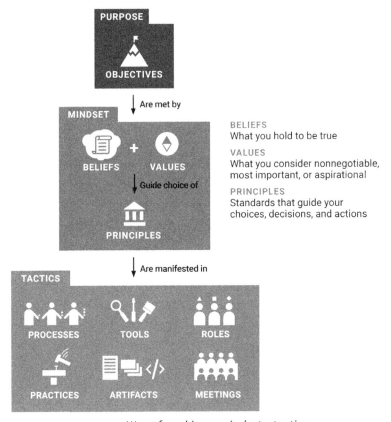

Way of working = mindset + tactics

As you take these steps, the following tips will be helpful:

Don't jump too far. Having used this strategy with many organizations, I've noticed that it generates a lot of excitement. Leaders love the potential of a new way of working, and they want it all: fast delivery cycles, frequent feedback, adaptive planning, engaged teams, collaboration everywhere, and on and on. In essence, they have a vision for Fitness Level 5. While that's good to have, it's also important to respect the staff's capacity for change and the leaders' capacity and ability to facilitate it.

Aim for progress, not perfection. When designing a way of working, it's natural to think "what if this happens? What if that happens?" Avoid the trap of trying to cover every eventuality. Expect that the choices you make now will inevitably evolve as the system's fitness increases (and as your plans meet reality). Another reason not to aim for perfection is that it's impossible: every choice has downsides. Want regular feedback? It takes time to process and apply. Want specialization? Even experts can and do make mistakes. Make choices that, *for now*, are likely to deliver enough upside and not much downside.

Simplify. Use the least amount of process and administration necessary at this point.

Consider options. There are many well-known ways to define a workflow, to organize a multi-team environment, to define roles and responsibilities, and so on. You can draw inspiration from them so you don't start from scratch. At the same time, be careful not to assume that popular off-the-shelf options are universally ideal; any so-called "best practice" can be a poor idea in certain contexts, including yours. Review all the tactical choices you consider for fit with your system's intended mindset (more on this below).

Work with your organizational reality. The recommendations you'll read below make a hidden assumption: nothing is out of bounds, and you can set up the system in the most promising way for achieving its goals. However, if your company is like most, some things are not going to change, and may not even be discussable. Examples I see all the time include the reporting structure, using sprints for the planning cycle, and having steering committees. Do what you can within the organization's self-imposed constraints, and try to get them reduced over time.

Head of Transformation at a bank:

"One of the most refreshing conversations I had was an agreement that 'nothing should be off the table by

default' if it would drive accelerated value delivery (obviously within regulation and risk appetite)."

Document the choices and decisions and the why behind them. Write everything down, briefly and clearly, in a single document and keep it in a central place. Assume people will misunderstand, forget, question, or be confused about some of the choices, so capture them accordingly. In the client examples I recount below, leaders stayed away from listing bullet points, using full sentences instead to make sure their intent was clear.

Step 1: Determine values and beliefs

The first and most important step is to determine what the system should value ("optimize for") as it works, and to articulate the assumptions that justify these values. Put another way, identify what is vital for the system to deliver the right product/solution to the right customer at the right time, and why these are your answers.

Facilitate a collaborative workshop with system leaders to work through this matter. Start it by making sure you're all on the same page about what the system needs to be like if it's highly fit for its purpose. To use the terms you encountered in Chapter 1: be explicit, and achieve alignment and consensus, about the optimum for each fitness aspect. Do that by discussing forward-looking, open questions about the aspects. Consider using the following questions and other ones that are relevant to your context (if needed, replace the term "product" with your equivalent, such as "service" or "solution").

- What types of outcomes does our product achieve and for whom?
- What would be most helpful for ensuring that we achieve these outcomes?
- What parts of the product are complex to define, develop, or deliver, and what's needed for dealing with that complexity effectively?

- What can we know and what should we decide about our product early on?
- How would innovation play a part in our success?
- In what ways would early or frequent delivery be beneficial to the customers/users and to us? What challenges would it create?
- What changes are likely in our business and technical landscapes that we'd need to adapt the product and/or the system to?
- Will development of the product materially end at some point, and what might happen afterwards?
- Where should we focus on progress, and where should we strive for perfection?
- In what ways do dates matter to delivery, and what is the cost profile of delaying past those dates?
- What are the benefits and downsides of having the same team both develop and maintain the product? And of having different teams?
- Given the scale of the value delivery system and its product, how might we decompose work (both conceptually and technically) to maximize system fitness?
- In which components or aspects of the product should we ensure uniformity, and where would it be better to let teams make local choices?
- What aspects of the way of working would be good to standardize?

Often, leaders already have some answers in mind, so this discussion shouldn't take long. The gold is in verbalizing and refining the answers, discussing differences, and reaching alignment. Having the discussion also strengthens the leaders' sense of sharing responsibility for improving fitness.

The next step in the workshop is to interpret and synthesize, from these perspectives, what the group thinks is important for success (the values) and why they think so (the beliefs). You might follow this up by inviting a wider set of less senior leaders to review and comment. Ultimately, reduce the values to the top three to five and the beliefs to less than a page.

A bank started a two-year, 35-person, eight-figure program: building a platform to consolidate financial transaction data from 30 globally distributed source systems. After finishing the relatively simple first phase, the director asked me to help with the longer and more complex second phase. I facilitated collaborative meetings in which 14 key people designed their approach to phase two. The participants reached agreement that the following were the phase's top values:

1. Data quality (accuracy, completeness, etc.)
2. Finishing the phase within nine months
3. Responding to changing, uncertain, or vague requirements
4. Platform quality

They also articulated some of their beliefs, of which the following had the highest impact on the design of the way of working:

- It's very hard to determine the right data from each source system — many are in other countries, their data isn't always clean, and there's a language barrier between us and the people who maintain them.
- Unless our platform brings in clean and complete data, downstream consumers won't use it.

- We can and should produce a complete spec for the platform, even though it will evolve.
- We know which source systems are in scope now, but others might be added later.
- It's both valuable and practical to complete the work for just a few source systems at a time.

You'll be done, for now, with the list of values and beliefs when most people feel confident that given what they know, these choices would maximize the chance of success.

Note: Across the company, you might have several value delivery systems, each of which evolves along its own path over time. Elicit values and beliefs for each system separately, and don't be surprised if they come out different. It's likely, however, that there is (or that the company wants there to be) a common denominator across the systems. In many companies nowadays that common denominator includes customer-centricity, quick response to change, frequent value delivery, and perhaps more. Still, be sure to conduct the activity described above; don't expect the common denominator to be the complete answer to what a specific system should optimize for.

Step 2: Choose operational principles

The next step is to pick operational principles that embody these values and beliefs. The principles describe how to choose work that counts, the approach to delivering value, the variables to manage as the work progresses, and the human environment in which all this takes place. This step is usually easy, as by now folks have made some mental image of how they'll approach work, and they're making that image more vivid.

Remember that principles permeate the system; they are not specific to individual functions. Even though people's activities may be quite different, they ought to apply the same principles as they carry them out. For instance, the principle "first be effective, then be efficient" means that everyone in the system should first be able to identify the right problems and produce the right solutions, and then strive to reduce the expense of doing so. To designers, that may mean seeking user feedback on low-fidelity designs; to developers, using test-driven development; to testers, conducting risk-based testing.

Following are examples of principles to prompt your thinking. As they come from diverse operational models, some principles contradict others. Always make sure your set is self-consistent, congruent with the chosen values and beliefs, and viable in your context.

- Make decisions with cross-functional consensus if they have a significant product impact.
- Base product-related decisions on intended outcomes, assumed cost of change, and cost of delay.
- Rely on internal staff (not on contractors or vendors) for developing parts where we want to preserve knowledge after the project ends.
- Use short time-boxes for *every* activity. Within time-boxes, work on the highest-impact things.
- Measure twice, cut once *(or the equivalent in tech-speak)*.
- Where domain or technical specialization is critical, let a few people become those specialists, and minimize their other work.
- Transparency: provide easy access to the information that guides decisions and actions.
- Avoid having any single points of failure.
- Maximize each team's ability to complete value-adding deliverables with minimal delay. Treat everyone who touches those deliverables as an equal member of the team.

- Take the time to learn from both successes and failures and then to improve the way of working.

- Trust that people would act professionally and conscientiously, which includes raising flags as early as possible.

- If a task has any risk, collaborate on it.

- Keep a sustainable pace.

Don't worry if your list comes to 15 or 20 principles. If you have more, chances are some principles imply (subsume) others, so you can remove the latter. Try reading the list out loud as if you're telling a story; I've found this helps the participants get a feel for its completeness and applicability.

Make sure the set of principles describes not only the approach to work but also the human side of the system. Early on, discuss the following important component of that: when several people do related work, do you expect them to operate as a workgroup, team, or Agile team? These distinct setups have different interaction patterns and leadership dynamics:

- A workgroup has centralized work assignment, and its members (who are usually specialists) have individual goals and little interdependence.

- A team shares goals and ownership, and its interdependent members have complementary skills and abilities, feel committed to each other, and exhibit helpfulness and cooperation.

- An Agile team is oriented to delivering customer/business value and operates with the Agile mindset. It has greater autonomy, self-organization, and collaboration than a "regular" team. Some of the members are specializing generalists, and the team doesn't experience delays due to members having outside assignments.

I've been in many situations where leaders wanted to have teams, and the word was used everywhere, but folks were really operating as workgroups; this misalignment is not good for fitness. If you believe that teams (Agile or otherwise) are the right construct, make sure they have proper leadership support and accountability structures to maximize their chances of becoming great teams.

Step 3: Determine tactics

What remains is to decide about the tactical level: team structure and process. This can go one of three ways.

Scenario 1: An off-the-shelf process framework, for instance Scrum, Kanban, or SAFe, seems likely to implement the chosen mindset very well. In this case, take it, adding or adapting elements to fit your context.

> Following this strategy with the product company whose fitness journey is recounted in Appendix B, their chosen values ("What we want to consider most important from now on") were:
>
> - Customer productivity: help our users (both expert and non-expert) be productive.
>
> - Striving for simplicity: in both our product and our way of working, avoid and remove unnecessary complexity, pain, and frustration.
>
> - Taking action: make decisions quickly (preferably based more on data), test ideas, and learn from failures, and do all this from a place of responsibility and ownership.
>
> - Helping each other succeed: operate in teams that collaborate, work well together, create shared understanding, and feel safe to ask for what they need to succeed.

- Continuous improvement: regularly improve our product and ways of working.

Based on these values and their forward-looking beliefs (not included here), an appropriate choice was to use Scrum in each software team and Kanban in the content team. The software teams' lines of ownership were redrawn to better reflect the product strategy; as a result, some engineers moved to other teams, and a few product specialists became product owners. Lead engineers took on Scrum Master and team leadership duties.

Scenario 2: The mindset aligns well with a conceptual model or philosophy such as self-managing teams, Lean, or traditional project management, but available process frameworks wouldn't implement it well enough. In this case, design the structure and process based on your values, beliefs, and principles using ideas from that model or philosophy.

A university-based team was building an open-source data management product for the scientific community, which in turn contributed to its codebase. Agility made sense, but many months of attempting to use Scrum didn't result in an effective process. Following my assessment, they reorganized reporting lines and staff assignments, adopted a north star metric to guide portfolio management, created a single task board from requirements to delivery, and established WIP limits per workflow stage.

Scenario 3: The mindset doesn't align entirely with any well-known model or philosophy; perhaps it's a hybrid of some. In this case, design your tactics from scratch.

In the bank example in Step 1 above, the values and beliefs indicate agility mixed with considerable upfront thinking and commitment. The leaders opted for many Agile principles, but arranged the staff in a custom four-team structure:

- A data team of twelve business analysts and three testers, responsible for all aspects of data and interactions with source systems and downstream consumers
- An architecture team, consisting of architects and data modelers
- A core team, working in two streams, each implementing one source system and its necessary platform support at a time
- An assembly team, focused on integration, configuration, tooling, and deployment

They also defined an initial workflow with a six-week release cadence and three classification levels for source systems' data maturity (akin to incremental definitions of "done"). Inside each six-week cycle, the teams collaborated to get a small number of systems to their next level of data maturity.

In all three scenarios, the design of the team structure and of the process go hand in hand. You might start with a promising team topology, draft a process, and iterate; alternatively, you might first sketch the process, draft an enabling team structure, and iterate. Either way, for the design to be effective, every person should feel *inclusion safety*: they belong in their group or team, are comfortable being themselves around their colleagues, and feel valued and appreciated. If the level of psychological safety is high enough, determining the team structure through a process of self-selection (in which people choose their teams) can be effective.

Although team size matters, don't look for a universally ideal number of members. A team is too small if it can't finish its work as needed, which is a matter of skills and domain knowledge. It's too large if it can't operate cohesively, which is a matter of safety and interpersonal trust (and to a much lesser extent, of efficient communication between members). The width of this spectrum is highly contextual.

The larger the system, the more care you'd need to take with the overall team structure or topology and with the exact composition of each team. At scale, watch for inter-team dependencies, delays, and coordination, as they exert the most weight on the system. Take into account Conway's Law's suggestion that the system would create a product architecture that corresponds to its communication structure. There are multiple ways to "scale" value delivery, all of which have different advantages and disadvantages and whose success hinges on different assumptions. Be sure to consider all those ways objectively, including the option of "de-scaling": decomposing the system into two or more. Although they wouldn't be entirely independent, each might have better fitness than the single big one.

The structure must also reflect how each manager supports the system's success. A common pitfall is to focus only on the technical teams, which leaves many managers assuming it's business as usual for them. The chosen arrangement must provide appropriate management of work and effective leadership of individuals and teams to be sustainable. Even more critical for the system's fitness, the people at the helm of the system should act as a team from the get-go, with explicit mission, values, principles, and working agreements.

SUPPLEMENTARY RESOURCE: Download "Steps to Designing a Team Process" from the book's companion website, DeliverBetterResultsBook.com.

Executing this strategy

Following the three-step process outlined above will likely require several meetings spread out over a couple of weeks. Make sure to include a good cross-system representation, and be particularly inclusive of and open to people who are nervous or doubtful about changing the status quo. Assume many people have questions or concerns; now is the time to articulate and discuss them.

This process produces an *initial* way of working. Whether its tactics are off-the-shelf or custom, you'll need to put it through its paces and iterate on it. You won't get it entirely right the first time; your human, organizational, and work contexts are too complex for that. It will change *anyway* as you apply later-level strategies.

You might find that naming your way of working — not referring to it merely as "our process" — draws people's interest and attention. Be careful though, because every name has connotations. Specifically, if the mindset aligns partly or fully with the Agile philosophy, *calling* it Agile might cause tension. After more than 20 years in play and many challenged "transformations," the name has baggage. You might have colleagues who are allergic to the word, conflate it with Scrum or with another specific framework, or are concerned that the chosen mindset isn't 100% what the Agile Manifesto says. Some companies refer to their ways of working using other terms, such as "value-driven," "adaptive," or "iterative."

Heading into implementation of the chosen way of working, a common risk is that the tactics look similar enough to the current ones that folks don't realize (or believe) that much is changing. As a result, both workers and front-line managers might feel that the whole initiative is nothing more than a managerial exercise. Choose your messaging carefully to communicate what *is* changing and how, what *isn't*, and the reasons for both.

And then there's the opposite risk: it's all very new for people. In that, Strategy 1b is different from the other nine in this book, which are incremental or evolutionary; this one may truly transform the way of working. That can be harder to lead, but you can't avoid it; if the structure, process, or their underlying mindset are fundamentally incompatible with the system's aim, iterating away from them in many tiny steps is not practical. Instead, gradually reach the strategy's target state by adopting both mindset and tactics *at the same time*. Do not roll out practices, processes, and tools and expect that over time, people would infer and embrace the mindset that makes their usage effective. This approach, though very common, has a poor track record of creating a fundamental change in choice-making, because mindset trumps tactics. Be sure to rely on advocates and ambassadors (see Chapter 3) — possibly numbering up to 10% of the staff.

As with all the strategies described in the book, this one needs to remain in play when the system reaches higher levels of fitness. This means keeping a watchful eye on the team structure and processes and ensuring they're appropriate for the system's intended purpose. Generally, you wouldn't need to repeat the design process outlined above unless the values and beliefs needed to change significantly, for example due to a business strategy pivot or because they turn out to be wrong. You should, however, expect drift: the tactics gradually straying away from alignment with the intended mindset. Drift often results from actions by newly hired managers and from uninformed local process fixes. I recommend that every few months, you assess the alignment together with team and management representatives; this will also serve as an opportunity to call fresh attention to this matter.

Another part of keeping this strategy in play, especially at higher levels of fitness, is to enhance or change some people's roles and responsibilities. Often, this happens in response to their wanting to advance, to changes in the needs from the system, or to the requirements of the higher-level strategies. The common denominator is that those folks' current roles and responsibilities are no longer a great fit for themselves or for the system.

> At a company progressing from Level 2 to 3, the single director of engineering (who had spent most of his time coding) became a technical director, in charge of the architecture but no longer of the team leads. The founder, to whom almost everyone had reported, became the head of design. Other people shifted into team leadership and product management positions.
>
> At another company on Level 3, the development managers and the QA manager no longer looked after their respective functions, and instead moved to manage cross-functional teams. This change began as a management team experiment. After some initial anxiety and skepticism, they found that it worked so well, they made the change permanent.

This strategy will have "done its part" for taking the system to Level 2 once the chosen mindset is appropriate for the goals of the system, and the structure and processes sustainably and viably implement that mindset.

 SUPPLEMENTARY RESOURCE: Go to DeliverBetterResultsBook.com and download "Steps to Designing a Team Process."

CHAPTER 6

PROGRESSING FROM LEVEL 2 TO 3

At Level 2, senior leaders collaboratively manage the project portfolio or roadmap for outcomes and capacity, and the system's way of working (structure, processes, and choice-making) is appropriate for the mission and objectives.

The system addresses the needs of management, customers, and stakeholders, but not effectively and efficiently enough. As a result, some of those needs produce interference, unplanned work, scope creep, frequent priority changes, escalations, and aborted work. These disruptions constantly threaten the applicability of the way of working, and therefore pose the highest risk to the system's continued fitness. In fact, unless leadership continues to keep the portfolio under control and the way of working aligned to purpose, both may drift enough to drop the system's fitness back to Level 1.

Now, the two strategies that will level up the system are to establish clear and appropriate decision-making and to stabilize the system. The former increases order in the system and the reliability of moving work through it, and the latter brings the variation in its performance into an acceptable range. Together, they resolve the abovementioned issues and ensure that it consistently produces satisfactory results.

STRATEGY 2A: SORT OUT DECISION-MAKING

In every value delivery system, people have titles, roles, and responsibilities. Yet, at Level 2, there tends to be a particular gap in decision-making that impacts the definition, development, and delivery of the product/solution: who makes some decisions, when, and how is unclear, inconsistent, or not fully defined. This directly affects all aspects of fitness for purpose.

For example, in many companies I've visited, the following questions didn't have definite answers:

- Given business/product priorities and technical considerations, who determines the *sequence* of work?
- How much detail should UX designers specify, and what can be left to developers to decide?
- Who decides that a feature is ready to go to production?
- Who can move a release date midway through development?

If your system has been growing quickly in size, this gap is likely obvious; leaders would notice that some decision-making is no longer appropriate or can't remain implicit. However, if your system's human composition has been stable, this "decision-making debt" is likely to be a blind spot.

This blind spot may exist whether you've organically evolved your way of working or adopted an off-the-shelf process framework. The emphasis has likely been on team-level processes and responsibilities, while folks in decision-making positions have seen little change in their job descriptions or in their managers' expectations. For example, Scrum and some of its related scaling frameworks are very clear about product ownership, but in many implementations, product owners still follow instructions from steering committees, VPs, and sponsors (who don't always speak with a single voice).

The decision-making gap exists also on the technical side. Several clients, when I started working with them, weren't clear and consistent about making architectural decisions. Sometimes senior developers made them, sometimes several tech leads collaborated and achieved consensus, and sometimes directors delivered a ruling.

Wherever the decision-making scheme has gaps, people who need to make progress will play it safe and follow cultural norms. In a control culture, they'll wait for their direct managers to make the calls; in an empowerment or ownership culture, they might go ahead with their own individual choices; in a consensus-heavy culture, they might call meetings for little matters. Relying on cultural norms will become more viable once your system gets to Level 4 or 5, but right now it might not produce the results you need.

Strategy 2a fills the gap in a straightforward manner: for every product-affecting decision, gain clarity and acceptance on who makes it and how.

> A startup prided itself on being product-led. To support their rapid growth, they executed Strategy 1b by forming "pods." Each pod had a dedicated product manager and a technical lead, and a single engineering director oversaw all the pods. The pods used Scrum tactics, while the product managers bore the duties normally associated with Scrum Masters.
>
> Product Development reached Fitness Level 2, but couldn't improve further. After a couple of months, the reason became apparent. Most product managers had scant Agile knowledge, so their process decisions weren't effective. As well, process administration ate into their availability for making product decisions. The company addressed this by promoting and hiring Agile team leaders to take on the process- and team-related responsibilities and later added engineering managers.

Articulating an explicit decision-making arrangement is a form of setting boundaries. As explained in Chapter 3, that's a good thing: people will have clarity and operate with agency, and they'll make the decisions that are on them to make.

None of this implies that decision-making needs to be in the hands of single people, who exercise positional authority or seek buy-in. Many decisions should rest with groups. In these cases, the groups should have effective and efficient methods for making their decisions.

Choosing who should own decisions

The way most organizations approach decision-making is by defining roles and responsibilities. A common artifact for that is the RACI matrix, which identifies who is Responsible, Accountable, Consulted, and Informed for each activity or deliverable.[1] People can then infer what needs to happen for a given decision — but only if they know everyone else's set of responsibilities. In my experience, this expectation doesn't scale well across a system, and the approach itself invites individualistic rather than team-based choices.

Another risk with this approach is that it's silent on the *decision* side of some responsibilities. Take, for example, the practice of code review. In most teams, conducting it is an explicit responsibility of the technical lead, a senior engineer, or fellow members, but who decides what to do about high-impact findings? I've met many teams that never answered this question, thus defaulting to "whatever the reviewer says goes." On one such team, the senior developer used the code review mechanism to cause the development of capabilities that the product owner hadn't meant to put on the backlog. They realized what was going on only after several features turned out to take double their estimated effort due to code-review rejections.

Clarity on roles and responsibilities is necessary in any system. With this strategy, you'll go further by explicitly asking:

For each decision we need to make for successful value delivery, who should make it and how?

In addition to increasing order in the system and the reliability of moving work through it, you'll shift the focus of discussion from specific people's authority and influence to the system and its work. As a result, you'll increase trust and collaboration and reduce risk.

Support the system's leaders in working (ideally collaboratively) through the above question. They should base the choice for each decision on the system's intended mindset, as determined in Level 1 (and perhaps refined since then). For example:

- If the system optimizes for frequent delivery by minimizing task delays, let many task-advancing decisions be made by team members. If some tasks require reviews or approvals, enable more people to provide them.

- If the system favors iterative and incremental work as a way to deliver more of the right and less of the wrong, consider having triads of product/business, design, and development leads break features down into smaller meaningful deliverables.

- If the system consists mostly of specialized, expensive experts and needs to use their time economically, a single person may orchestrate their tasks.

If the system has been leaning toward greater staff ownership and team orientation, there might be friction with people who have formal authority over team members. Reduce the tension and the potential for mixed messages by being explicit about decisions that might be assumed to flow top-down. Examples I've helped facilitate include:

- Choosing the work for the next week or two requires a collaborative discussion among team members and the product manager. The engineering manager supports the team but doesn't assign work directly to individuals.

- Determining the ship date during release planning is the product manager's call (based on input from others), but changing the date afterwards requires cross-functional consensus, including from technical managers.

> At a fast-growing startup (Fitness Level 2), "who makes product decisions" was a source of high tension. Despite the VP's earnest attempts to empower the product managers (PMs), they had little say over features; the two founders — who were the CEO and COO — decided everything. Helping them work through their mistrust of the PMs and allow the PMs to grow on the job took months.

Your environment might default to putting decision-making in the hands of managers. For some decisions, that might be the best choice — even if it's actually driven by habit or the org chart — while for others it might limit fitness. The best choices align with the system's intended values, beliefs, and principles, because then it can operate coherently.

I've found it best to make decision assignments in collaborative, cross-functional workshops, because participants keep each other honest about the intended mindset, and because senior managers don't want to appear aggressive.

Many process options are available to help a *group* make a decision. Soliciting input, reviewing comments, synthesizing options, and finalizing choices can each take place synchronously (in a meeting) or asynchronously. To finalize choices, they may seek consensus or defer to a leader in the group.

Just like the workflow and team structure, decision-making arrangements should not be fixed for all time. They should evolve as value delivery fitness improves or conditions change.

When I started working with the digital department of a media organization, it was two years into a Scrum transformation and the fitness level was 2. A few of the ten teams needed help creating effective decision-making arrangements due to personality clashes.

At Level 3, leadership worked hard to create psychological safety and enable collaboration. As well, decision-making became heavily based on consensus: everyone had a chance to be involved and heard, and was committed to follow through with decisions (it didn't mean that everyone loved each decision or that it had to be watered down).

Once the department's fitness reached Level 4 — and had grown the headcount by 50 percent — the consensus mechanism was clearly slowing them down. The leadership team identified two categories of decisions that could be made by small, self-selecting groups without requiring wider consensus: one that groups could make entirely on their own, and another that would require a nod from senior management.

Executing this strategy

Start by making an inventory of high-impact decisions that need to be sorted out, along with the consequences of the status quo. Use that to give system leaders visibility into the "decision debt" and understanding of its significance. Alternatively, host a workshop with the leaders to produce that inventory together; even though the activity is probably unfamiliar, doing it in a group should be quick and easy.

Ideally, include in the inventory decisions that already have a home, but that home could be revisited with the benefit of hindsight. I say "ideally" because doing this may not be safe or welcome (yet).

Working through the inventory, help the leaders choose who should make which decisions (or types of decisions) and how. If your system's way of working is based on a popular process framework or methodology, consider its answers but be open to adapting them to your context. Doing all this will likely take place in multiple meetings spread out over weeks. Treat some of the higher-impact choices as experiments: try them for a while, evaluate the outcomes they produce, adjust as needed, repeat. Document everything in an easily accessible place and communicate the choices across the system.

If your intent is to have teams own more decisions than they're used to, find out whether they're willing to own them and able to make good ones. If that's not the case, seek to understand the reasons (remember to use system thinking). For example, if they're comfortable being told what to do, why is that, and what's keeping this pattern in place? None of this invalidates the intent to increase team ownership of decisions, but you might need to make a few changes or use transitional solutions before implementing it fully.

As you carry out this strategy, you'll focus mostly on decisions that directly affect the product. Along the way, you'll likely identify a need to work on decision-making that *indirectly* affects it, such as around process management and hiring. Some of that will probably stem from incomplete or ineffective choices made while executing Level 1 strategies.

As time goes on, you'll probably run into situations that didn't occur to you initially. A common example in empowered environments is the "shoulder tap" scenario: when a senior manager identifies important or urgent work that's not on any team's current plan, they approach an individual contributor and task them with it. That tends to be disruptive to the system, so a determination is needed: who decides what to do about such work?

Another common scenario is that people who own a decision no longer want it or don't make it well enough. On one IT project, the product owner was fully on top of his responsibilities, but after several months in the role, realized that he didn't understand the system enough to manage the backlog effectively. The project leaders tapped a virtual team of five managers and business people to make backlog decisions using majority vote. The project's results improved following the change, and the person was happy to leave the PO role.

This strategy will have "done its part" to get your system to Level 3 when decision-making is appropriate, timely, and harmonious enough to move the product forward without reversing or changing course unnecessarily.

STRATEGY 2B: STABILIZE THE SYSTEM

With Strategy 1a (manage the project portfolio) in place, the system's workload doesn't exceed its capacity. Now, let's turn our attention to how the system deals with that workload.

Our first aim is to make the system *stable*. It is stable when a sustainable balance exists between the demands on one side and the supply (outputs) on the other end. That means the system is reliable: you can have **realistic expectations** about the range of time and quality for delivery of features, experiments, projects, and other portfolio items.

I've emphasized the words **realistic expectations** because the business world loves predictability. However, no value delivery system can have predictability in the mathematical or physical sense. Every system's output fluctuates, in part due to inherent variation ("common causes" or "noise") and in part due to special causes that the system isn't set up to handle.

You'll need to correctly identify special causes and address important recurring ones. Then, this section's many recommendations will help you to reduce and shift the range of inherent variation enough so it's also *acceptable* from the perspective of the system's fitness for purpose.

There's a caveat, though. The above makes the hidden assumption that the demand — the projects, features, defects, and other things your system needs to work on — retains its current scope and arrival rate. But what if the demand grows substantially? Trying to fulfill all of it will produce the consequences you experienced when the system was at Level 1. It'd be better, as part of your portfolio management activities, to reject the least valuable and least strategic demand to prevent overburdening. However, if that's not an option, you'll need to grow the system to take on the additional work. Revisit Strategies 1b (design the way of working) and 2a (sort out decision-making) to ensure that both are appropriate for the bigger system, and then turn your attention to stabilizing it.

The stability of your system will look different depending on its planning cycles and release lengths. For example:

- If teams work on projects that take several months, the projects move reliably through the pipeline. They can be started around their expected time, they don't miss their due dates too much, and rework (which interferes with new projects) is low.
- If teams plan and deploy releases quarterly, their plans work out acceptably well in reality.
- If teams work in cycles of two to four weeks, whether as part of projects or not, their throughput per cycle is distributed within an acceptable range.
- If teams work in flow (processing and delivering a few work items at a time, whether as part of projects or not), their lead times from commitment to delivery are distributed within an acceptable range.

Creating system stability is important for several reasons. Delivering items in a more-timely manner is valuable to customers. Everyone who depends on these deliveries can plan more reliably, and estimates and forecasts become more viable; without stability, dates on your roadmap are merely wishful thinking. There's less of the stress and overhead associated with managing unstable systems (think escalations, tension with stakeholders, and endless status reporting). And, it's a prerequisite for the Level 3 and 4 strategies for even greater fitness for purpose.

How *not* to stabilize a system

If your system can't reliably meet the demand placed upon it, you have many options to deal with the situation. Let's first examine some that are well-intended and familiar but *tricky*: though they may be partly useful sometimes, executing them regularly or maximally compromises various fitness aspects and doesn't increase stability. Use them judiciously and situationally.

Make detailed plans by identifying all the tasks upfront. It's important to understand the work's outcomes, risks, and dependencies before starting it. However, going much deeper reduces adaptability, and is more wasteful when some choices turn out to be wrong.

Optimize schedules by preparing precise estimates. While understanding the magnitude of work is often useful, spending time on trying to prepare precise estimates reduces the available time for working on outcome-yielding deliverables. As with the previous option, that's harmful and wasteful to the extent the estimates are proven wrong. Estimates also tend to create an illusion of certainty (you know how quickly they can become commitments) and therefore produce even greater consequences for being wrong. If estimation becomes an unsafe activity, people pad the numbers to protect themselves, planning is no more accurate, and the system is no more stable than before.

Maximize workers' output by using up their entire available time. This option is also known as "keeping people fully loaded" and "resource efficiency." Having people take on additional work is helpful to the extent that it doesn't clog the pipe and make it harder for the entire system to deliver results. Having folks take on *more* than that might be useful in special cases, but in the aggregate it creates delays, pushes out deliveries, and compromises quality.

Increase capacity temporarily by doing overtime. Most people in value delivery can do this only for short periods of time and as a rare exception; more than that is not sustainable. As well, the greater the overtime, the greater the reduction in quality. As a talented developer told me once, "Around 5 pm is when I start writing the bugs I'll have to fix tomorrow."

Increase capacity long-term by enlarging the team. While this may be a good response to real growth in demand, it may result in a short-term hit to quality and productivity. Managing a larger team — or, if you split it, a few smaller ones — can present additional challenges.

How to stabilize a system

Portfolio items usually move through the system in pieces, generically called **work items**. Depending on the process, some of these work items might be tasks (such as for specification, design, and coding) and some might be end-to-end portions of the portfolio item. Each work item may take a small number of people anywhere from hours to a few weeks of touch-time, with its duration (clock time) possibly being much longer. Most work items go through a similar *workflow* through a few functions, teams, or individuals. Taken together, the system's workflows describe how it turns portfolio items into deliveries.

Given that your system's fitness has passed Level 1, its team structure and workflows are appropriate for its needs. Stabilizing it, therefore, is a matter of improving choice-making regarding the work items. This section offers ideas and principles, which have stood the test of time, for doing that. Many of them come from Kanban and Agile methods, although they're also useful for more plan-driven methods. This is a long list, but you *don't have to use all of them*, certainly not from the get-go.

Visualize the work. To make effective decisions about moving work through the system, you have to see where all the work is and what's happening to it. The previous chapter recommended doing so for the portfolio, and the same concept applies at the level of work items. The typical artifact for this is a board (whether physical or electronic): columns represent workflow stages, and items move from left to right as they proceed through the workflow. It's often useful to subdivide boards horizontally into "swimlanes" to call out different classes of items, such as new value-adding work, defects, and improvements.

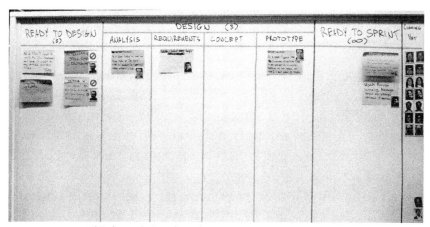

*This board visualizes how a certain system's work
flows from committed idea to development*

It's a little harder to manage boards at this level than at the portfolio level, due to the number of items and workflow stages across different functional areas, but the concept is equally powerful. Proper visualization reinforces the "watch the work, not the workers" philosophy and enables making prompt and intelligent decisions about items. It helps decision-makers stabilize the system by making visible several risks to stability, such as items aging or being blocked, bottlenecks, and exceeding of intended limits.

This board visualizes that system's subsequent flow of work in development

Define explicit intake and completion standards. Every system has a degree of *rework*: requirements and specifications to rethink, designs to correct, code to fix, migrations to retry, etc. In cases where people can't or won't get stuff perfect the first time, incurring certain rework may be economical and strategic. For example, a throwaway prototype is worth producing if it teaches important real-world lessons. In other cases, rework is preventable and wasteful. The effect on stability arises not from the rework itself but from its *variability*: the higher it is, the less stable the system.

One easy way to reduce preventable rework and its variability is to define standards or policies for moving items from one workflow stage to the next. It's often helpful to capture such standards as checklists that reflect the item's readiness for the next stage. In a common example, a definition of "Ready" may help a development team ensure that they have everything they need to start working on a feature/story (note: this doesn't mean they work from perfect requirements; the item might be experimental or evolutionary). In another common example, a definition of "Done" may include criteria that a feature/story has to satisfy before it can be deployed.

Cultivate learner safety. If people are to do their job properly, they should feel safe to ask for clarifications, say "We don't know," study what they need, try things out, and own up to mistakes. Without this kind of safety, their actions are likely to result in a high level of rework. Help leaders *throughout the system* to establish learner safety. Notice the emphasis: this isn't an issue for the technical teams alone. Their managers and business counterparts — who are also members of the system — also need to experience learner safety. For more advice on cultivating safety, see Chapter 7.

Increase intrinsic quality. If the product's design and construction are poor or hard to work with, developing new features is risky. Extensive testing and rework — having potentially high variability — might be needed to ensure that new features are ready to ship and that existing ones aren't broken. Additionally, any breakage discovered in production places urgent demand on the system and interferes with other work.

To make system stability possible, you must take two separate but not-unrelated actions. One is to improve areas of the product's design and construction where further development is particularly problematic. This action usually requires breaking down, decoupling, or even replacing large components. The second action is to enhance the testing approach to catch breakage early and efficiently, usually with the help of automated checks.

The matter of intrinsic quality also applies to the artifacts used in the making of the product, such as specs, user stories, test plans, and internal-facing documentation. If they are inconsistent, ambiguous, or disorganized, their users — the system's people — might make unnecessary mistakes, whose effect on the system's stability is hard to predict. Ask various individual contributors which artifacts tend to worry them, and upgrade their structure and related processes.

Break work down into smaller meaningful pieces. This staple of Agile thinking speaks to determining and sequencing the work items that build up to a portfolio item. In Agile, the idea is to deliver the portfolio item in an iterative and incremental (evolutionary) sequence of work items that produce mini-outcomes. That's different from decomposing the portfolio item into a sequence of functional tasks, because each would likely still be big and the risky part (integration) happens at the end.

In addition to early value delivery and easier adaptation, this principle contributes to stability in two ways. One, it helps reduce and isolate dependencies between work items. Two, it prevents big work — which always takes longer than you hope — from clogging up the pipe. You'll achieve these effects already by decomposing large work into medium work; the pieces don't have to be tiny.

You'll also benefit from this principle if you work on a months-long, non-Agile project: sequence the work so you deliver something every month. By dividing the problem up and testing as you go, you'll reduce two major late-stage risks: big surprises and scope creep.

Get to "done" (finish what's started). Even if you limit how many tasks are *actively* in progress, having a pile of started-but-waiting ones impacts overall reliability. Do what you can to finish what's started with minimal delays; don't let items age too much. If you also apply the above mentioned principle of breaking work down, get to "done" on each piece.

Reduce bottlenecks. A bottleneck occurs when incoming work overwhelms the people performing a step in the workflow. As more of it piles up, the system slows down and its variability grows (you know this phenomenon from traffic jams). Two effective responses suggested by the Theory of Constraints[2] are:

1. Make better use of people's time and of the tools at the bottleneck by offloading some of their other obligations. For example, if your star developer doesn't have enough time for coding the most complex features, perhaps she can reduce the time she spends on code reviews and candidate interviews.

2. Modify the process to reduce dependency on the bottleneck. For example, if code deployments are delayed because the Security team always has too much code to check, they might build or configure tools for the development teams to perform some of the security checking on their own.

Constrain work intake. Impose artificial constraints so that teams and individuals avoid taking on more work than they can realistically complete. Two useful and popular constraints, which may be combined but don't have to be, are:

1. Plan work and execute it in small time-boxes. The team determines a short duration, and plans by asking, "What's the best thing we can do in this time-box?" When the time-box ends (or optionally sooner), they plan the next cycle. Two common examples of this are sprints and release trains.

2. Limit work-in-process (WIP). The team determines a low number, and never works on more items than that at a given time. When they find themselves with fewer items in flight, they may take in more, up to the limit, though they'd do better to finish most of the ones in flight. It's often helpful to have different WIP limits on individual workflow stages, especially if different teams and specialists work on them.

Terminology note: You might have heard that the acronym WIP stands for "work in *progress*." While not wrong, this term connotes that all work is in fact progressing toward completion. "Work in *process*" (the original term) encompasses work that's anywhere in the pipe — including work that's blocked or waiting — and is therefore more accurate for the purposes of managing flow.

Time-boxes need to be short enough, and WIP limits low enough, to produce effects that increase the system's stability. One such effect is the encouragement of people to focus, break work down, and collaborate — behaviors that make items flow more smoothly through the pipe. Another effect is the replacing of the "push" approach — the default in product development — with a "pull" one. In "push," people who complete the workflow stage for a given item move it to the next stage whether it has room for the item or not. In "pull," people take an item into a workflow stage when they have the capacity to perform that stage's activity. A third effect is the reduction of high-variability delays that result from excessive context switching.

The challenge with these *enabling constraints* on work intake is the trust they require. The ideal WIP limit or time-box content might be small enough to make a manager worry, "Is my team busy enough?" — or to make a team worry that the manager thinks that. I've met many managers who were concerned that team members would misuse low WIP limits to make work light for themselves (which is much harder to do when the only limit is the implicit one of available work hours). To constrain work intake effectively, all parties must be clear on the purpose of this principle and to operate with explicit trust.

Turn as much unplanned work into planned work as possible. Even with solid management of priorities and intake, some demand will be placed on the system in the form of *unplanned work* (at Level 2, possibly quite a lot of it). Part of that demand is literally unplanned because the requesters don't think of it beforehand or try to bypass the intake mechanisms. There might even be a reinforcing loop here: they say their work items are urgent, the system scrambles to act on them at the expense of strategic work, and the requesters learn that "urgent" always bumps them to the front of the line — even when some requests are not actually urgent. Sometimes, explaining the consequences to people is enough to make a significant improvement; at other times, you'll need to make process changes.

Determine how to handle the rest of unplanned work. You really can't anticipate some types of demand, such as production outages, urgent customer requests, and security incidents. Categorize all this work and decide how to deal with each category.

> Some teams face production issues, support questions, and other interruptions often enough that they dedicate a developer to addressing them. The rest of the team tends to the regular work and to improving the state of production. The "firefighter" or "steward" rotates weekly, which increases the spread of knowledge in the team, reduces individuals' stress, and amplifies a sense of shared ownership.

Keep spare capacity. If everybody's time is always full with planned work, how will they deal with unplanned work? You know the likely answer: by pulling overtime, dropping important work, or cutting corners. In a vicious cycle, these behaviors create more unplanned work and waste, impacting the system's results. Make sure that *across the system*, individuals and teams keep enough spare cycles to deal with unplanned work while maintaining a sustainable pace. And whenever they don't put those spare cycles toward unplanned work, they engage in activities that indirectly produce value: improve the process, reduce technical debt, learn something, collaborate with colleagues. Like the enabling constraints on work intake, this one requires explicit trust between staff and management!

Manage high-variability delays. Collect data on how long work items take to get from start to finish, and see if any items take much longer than they should based on the actual touch time. Map out their flow, and you'll likely find periods of excessive waiting for experts, reviews, approvals, vendors, integration, testing, etc. All this waiting is bad for the system, but the specific impact to stability is not in the delays per se; it's when their occurrence and duration are not predictable enough. Identify those delays and deal with their causes. Some delays might be "the usual suspects," such as a team with excessive WIP. Others might be early in the workflow, such as at the point where management decides which portfolio items to bring forward or stop, if they make this decision too infrequently.[3]

Enable people to contribute outside narrow specialties. While having people take tasks in which they're experts has clear advantages, *always* doing that may create bottlenecks and delays, because experts tend to get overloaded. Not all tasks require deep specialization, so create opportunities for people to expand their repertoire and to contribute to finishing work.

SUPPLEMENTARY RESOURCE: Download the "How to Stabilize a Value Delivery System" quick reference guide from the book's companion website, DeliverBetterResultsBook.com.

Using process metrics

Your stabilization efforts may be more effective if you base them on data. For the most part, collect output data, not input data; in other words, focus on the system's production of deliverables, not on the busyness of its people. Be sure to measure both across the system *and* in some of its natural divisions, like teams. Specifically for stabilization, helpful metrics include:

1. Lead time: the time between accepting a request into the system and delivering on it

2. Cycle time: the time between certain points in the workflow (e.g., between entering a sprint backlog and being accepted by the product owner)

3. Throughput: the number of items delivered in a period of time (e.g., user stories delivered per day or week)

These metrics focus on items. Also collect process data on deployments to production, such as frequency, failures, and recovery.[4]

Each of these and other common metrics is usually calculated and discussed as a single number. However, it's actually a *distribution*, which is the important thing from a stability standpoint. To understand its variation, make a process behavior chart using the sequence of data points over time. Remember that variation within an expected range is inherent to the system ("noise"), while extreme data points are probably due to special causes that you should attend to. Beware the common management pitfall of taking corrective action with noise as if it has special cause; for example, if a team's average velocity is generally 20 points and last sprint they completed 17 points, intervening with an assumption that something's wrong may do more harm than good.

If your system relies on effort estimation for planning, also collect data on how long the items actually take. That reflects what the system is really like, rather than what people wish it were like or the biases that affect their estimates. To reduce the gaps between estimates and actuals, analyze the differences every few weeks (which would likely lead you to consider some of the principles and tactics listed in the previous section). Note: while performing this analysis is naturally useful in frequent-planning processes, it's also useful in processes that concentrate planning upfront.

The use of data comes with several warnings.

Collect and analyze data to discover opportunities to *improve the system*, not to micromanage, pressure, or compare people. Your mindset will come through in your choice and use of metrics, and people will respond to it. For example, if you try to assess individual productivity (say, by counting the number of code commits per person), developers might assume that their personal performance matters more than their team's, and would be less inclined to collaborate with teammates.

Remember that people respond to the environment they're in. Metrics that receive close management attention or that get shared too widely (even in the name of transparency) tend to influence people's behavior, and not always positively. For example, counting delivered items may lead some development teams to cut corners to avoid low numbers. This phenomenon is sometimes called "gaming the system," a term which connotes bad intentions even when there aren't any (people may be trying to make the best of a difficult situation). Make sure the collection, analysis, and subsequent actions don't compromise psychological safety.

> *"It is not the team that games the system, it is the system designer that creates the game."*
>
> — *Doc Norton, Head of Technology*
> *at Covered Insurance*

Get the story behind the numbers. In other words, don't jump to conclusions. If team A completes twice as many story points as team B and team C's velocity is erratic, don't think of B and C as underperforming; look into the system to understand what's going on. Also do that if the metrics are great! For example, if throughput looks good, it would behoove you to know if it's the result of great teamwork and process or of a couple of members' unsustainable heroism.

Avoid making the improvement of metrics a goal. Your goals should focus on improving the system's capabilities. If you do set a target for any metric (rather than merely look for variation and patterns), determine the target based on your own context. The point is not to achieve perfection or some industry average, it's to make the system stable and reliable, which will both increase its fitness for purpose and its readiness for further improvements.

Executing this strategy

Most of these system-management activities, whether proactive or reactive, don't require concentrated effort and time. What they do require is ongoing intention and attention. Therefore, it's often helpful to put the overall responsibility or stewardship of the matter in someone's hands. At a single team level, that's usually an engineering manager, team leader, or project manager. At the system level, it may be a program manager, a director, or someone else; the critical thing is to work system-wide, not on a functional subset. For example, increasing the reliability of delivery won't help much if the performance in design and development is all over the place.

Of the suggested techniques, start with visualizing the work. It's useful in any operational model; it also facilitates subsequent stabilization efforts and elevates their perceived importance. Gradually bring in some of the other techniques, based on progress and appetite. Monitor how the changes are working out, but don't just rely on hard data; also talk to people to understand where their work doesn't flow smoothly.

While executing this strategy, remember to keep the Level 1 strategies in play:

- Continue monitoring the chosen mindset, structure, and processes for suitability to their intended purpose. If some of those choices aren't turning out quite right, you'll need to make adjustments.

- Keep managing the portfolio collaboratively. You might discover that you need to be even stricter about limits on portfolio stages to stabilize the system.

A company with 500 people in R&D had an effective team structure and process. It managed the project portfolio implicitly via division of labor: some teams worked on a backlog for one chunk of the product, other teams worked on the platform, and so on. That was enough to achieve Level 2, as all the important work was getting the right attention. However, that important work usually touched many parts of the product, requiring people from multiple teams to coordinate efforts. Since these dependencies were not accounted for, the portfolio WIP was effectively too high, and the system couldn't be stabilized enough to make Level 3 possible. This also explains why Strategy 3a (increase safety, teamwork, and collaboration), which was in play across R&D, didn't raise the fitness level.

This strategy will have "done its part" to get your system to Level 3 when week to week, month to month, the variation in the system's output is acceptable. Staff members feel the regularity, and are not nervous about finishing their deliverables.

 SUPPLEMENTARY RESOURCE: Go to DeliverBetterResultsBook.com and download "How to Stabilize a Value Delivery System."

CHAPTER 7
PROGRESSING FROM LEVEL 3 TO 4

Assuming your system's fitness sits sustainably at Level 3, several matters are in place. Leaders collaboratively manage the project portfolio for outcomes and capacity. The system's structures and processes are appropriate for what's required of it. It is stable and reliable, and every decision that impacts the product or solution has a home. These are wins worth celebrating!

Overall, the system contributes satisfactorily to the achievement of company objectives. Of the six fitness aspects — throughput, outcomes, timeliness, adaptability, consistency, and cost-efficiency — one or two are close enough to their optimum to not be an issue. Likely, only one or two are of ongoing concern; usually, those are outcomes and adaptability.

The system's results, however, are almost entirely determined by the high-impact decisions made by a few people. Typically, those folks are product leads, architects or senior individual contributors, and middle managers — and they don't act as a team. Two unvoiced assumptions are shared throughout the system: the planned work equals the right work, and the potential improvement gains from collaboration aren't worth the time.

With a few people driving all important decisions, others feel poorly connected to the mission and to their customers. They are fully loaded "resources" that check tasks off, feeling like cogs in a machine. The machine is at risk, though, because it's optimized a certain way and its capacity to adapt to big changes is low.

Three strategies will now bring your system to Level 4 while improving its resilience. The first one unleashes human potential and synergy by increasing contributor safety, real teamwork, and collaboration. This strategy enables the next two, which enhance all aspects of fitness: deferring commitments and increasing release frequency, and engaging teams more meaningfully, collaboratively, and efficiently in planning.

STRATEGY 3A: INCREASE SAFETY, TEAMWORK, AND COLLABORATION

Your people perform the necessary work, almost all of them doing so in teams, and they cooperate. With Strategy 3a, which sits squarely on the human side of the system, you'll make it possible and welcome for them to engage and interact on a whole different level.

Contributor safety

In Level 1 you worked on inclusion safety: people feel valued and welcome in their group or team. In Level 2 you cultivated learner safety, and folks feel safe to ask for clarifications and to say "We don't know"; they have room to learn what they need to do their work, with the expectation that progress in learning involves some mistakes. Now is the time to go further and cultivate **contributor safety**: to enable everyone to be full participants in conceiving, making, and delivering the product.

Let's do a thought exercise in two parts. First, pick a system team that you know well. Are their planning meetings generally lively, and every opinion has a chance to be heard respectfully? In retrospectives, do members go beyond dry process matters and discuss personal concerns about the work? In planning or review meetings, do they sometimes push back on questionable ideas from managers or stakeholders? When discussing work status, are they upfront about problems, risks, and impediments? Can the team lead bring bad news to their director or VP?

Now consider the system at large. Can a developer coordinate a technical matter with a developer on a different team, without any tech leads or managers frowning upon that? Can a tester explore some product behaviors outside of her team's mandate? Can a product manager strategically leave the details of a new feature for later elaboration, and nobody would look upon that as unprofessional? Can a manager answer an executive's question with "I'll check with the team"?

If some of your answers fell short of "yes," that team or those individuals don't have enough *contributor safety*. Everyone works hard and takes part in their team's process, but they hold back. They probably avoid collaboration and early feedback for fear of judgment. They protect themselves, spending their efforts on what they think they're *supposed* to do (even if they officially have some autonomy) rather than what they think is right. As a result, they may not feel that they make enough of a difference.

The concept of psychological safety has two sides. The one described so far, which is the one that gets the most attention in knowledge-work leadership discussions, refers to the **safety to engage where others are involved**. When you're safe, you get a second chance if you mess up. You don't have free license to be negative or critical, but you can offer dissenting opinions. You manage your behaviors, but you don't have to be guarded. You communicate with more senior people about issues and risks with minimal filtering, but you won't lose your job if you do so with the interests of the company at heart. This side of safety is interpersonal and therefore cultural.

The other side is **safety to do one's work without fear of failure or trouble**. Can you recall instances where folks created problems without meaning to? Given the complexity and difficulty of the work, you probably don't have to go too far back to find examples, such as developers causing regressions in one area by changing code in another area, testers missing defects, designers complicating user journeys, and product managers misreading the importance of some features. To the extent that creating problems is easy and personally risky for workers, they'll direct their efforts to self-protection. But when the system makes it safe to work, folks can give their full attention to producing results. Enabling this side of safety is largely a matter of process: it should be designed to eliminate catastrophic failures and to minimize non-catastrophic ones.

> **This is basic practice in many other professions. For example, biological lab technicians wear protective clothing and follow standard operating procedures. At construction sites, safety features must be present and workers must wear specific personal protective equipment before they start working.**

There is always a gap between what people could *ideally* contribute to their team's and company's success and what they *actually* contribute. Safety plays a role in the size of the gap. Low safety breeds a "check the box" or order-taking mentality that keeps the system's fitness from rising past Level 3. Higher safety is a necessary condition for many fitness-increasing behaviors such as tolerating unknowns and ambiguity, experimenting when needed, and taking responsibility for customer-meaningful deliveries.

As mentioned in Chapter 3, the best way to use this book's advice is for various leaders, acting in partnership, to apply it throughout the system. That goes doubly so for safety, because it must be part of the culture, not dependent on individual leaders who may come and go. If team members and managers across the system perceive very different levels of safety, the system won't advance much.

The operative word in the previous sentence is "perceive." **Perceived safety** matters a lot more than **actual safety** and **intended safety**. As a leader, you might honestly believe you've created a safe environment, while the people who operate within it feel otherwise. In some cases, that's not about you at all; they experience (or believe they experience) threats from other leaders in the company. That's why partnering with other leaders across the system, and with the executives above it, is vital.

Enhancing the safety to engage

Across the business world, more and more managers (at all levels) are familiar by now with the concept of safety to engage. If some of your peers, executives, or stakeholders are not, help them advance their understanding of its significance. While you can do so by sharing books, videos, or posts on the topic, look for opportunities to broach the subject using actual examples from your environment. Two impactful ways of doing that are:

- If their relationship with one colleague is based on mutual commitment to shared purpose and values, while their relationship with another is a transactional dynamic of apportioning work and expecting accountability, help them see the impact of the different levels of safety on each person's results.

- When some success or failure occurs, try the "5 whys" technique. Ask why something happened, feed the answer into another "why?" question, continuing recursively like that for a total of five whys. In some cases, one of the answers along this causal chain is that people acted the way they did because of the level of safety they felt.

Others' safety, and your trust in them, are different but dependent matters: by increasing your trust, you increase their safety. You build both safety and trust through your **behaviors**: what you say and do, and what you don't say and don't do. To adopt desired behaviors effectively, build **habits** around them. The following three habits are powerful yet easy to create.

Habit 1: Pause. Before you take an action, pause, and ask yourself: "How might I be reducing safety?" For example:

- Are you thinking of nudging teams to improve their performance by sharing every team's "percent delivered vs. committed" metric in the next cross-team meeting? When I conducted an assessment for a client that did this, a team referred to it as public shaming! Assuming that teams keep using this metric, replace the open sharing with safer alternatives. For example, ask teams to take time in their retrospectives to analyze the root causes of trends or lower-than-expected percentages.

- Would you like to start joining daily team meetings, even as a silent observer, to show that you're involved? Some teams might doubt your intention and start censoring themselves in your presence (on each person's turn to speak, they'll say that everything's fine). Instead, consider having informal check-ins with team members. When they report issues that block them, work visibly to remove those impediments.

- Suppose that a project's status is regularly green. One day, a team member approaches you privately and shares their concern that the project is going to fall flat with customers. What might you say to them? Which of your reactions would dissuade the person from sharing other concerns with you in the future? And if that person is right, which of your reactions would make things unsafe for their colleagues?

Habit 2: Lead with curiosity, not blame. To paraphrase Deming, your system is perfectly designed to get the results that it gets — which includes performance problems and unwanted behaviors. If problems occur — even something as serious as a production outage — assume that what happened was a result of faults in the system. Guarantee safety to the people who "caused the problem" so they feel free to provide maximum information about their actions to aid the discovery of those faults. Meetings where such discovery is conducted are sometimes called "blameless retrospectives."

Habit 3: Critique, don't criticize. At Level 1, you determined the mindset — values, beliefs, and principles — that would maximize the system's success. If that mindset includes getting feedback on preliminary, quick, and incomplete work, make it safe for people to show such work. A powerful habit to borrow from the design world is this: comment on the work's merits and problems based on relevant professional principles, without making it personal.[1]

Safety, like trust and empowerment, is tested in times of trouble. Think ahead to likely problems and consider how you'd react. Better yet, discuss this explicitly with others and set explicit *norms*. Two examples of safety-related norms are "How we will resolve conflicts," and "How we'll discuss hard stuff."

Safety to engage takes time to build and little effort to destroy. But there's a silver lining, or an insurance policy if you will. If you're visibly intentional about creating safety — if you're explicit about your intents, you're transparent, you demonstrate vulnerability, you really trust people, you accept feedback respectfully, and so on — it will be relatively easy to recover from missteps. Use those missteps as an opportunity for creating or upgrading norms.

Enhancing the safety to work

As mentioned earlier, safety to work is largely enabled by process. Study your system's processes and identify points where people — even the most competent and well-meaning — may work unsafely. There's no shortage of these in software development: enhancing features, refactoring code, deploying to production, migrating databases, deprecating interfaces, sometimes even updating texts. Identify what might cause the riskiest and costliest points, and experiment with changes to make work safer (your teams may have great suggestions in this matter!). Possible solutions may include:

- Improving the quality of peer reviews and doing more work collaboratively
- Relying on artifacts such as checklists, standards, and documentation (while being careful not to stifle creativity and independent thought)
- Automating error-prone manual activities
- Running automated checks
- Adhering to architectural patterns

Another solution that tends to appear as companies grow large (but is also suitable for smaller ones) is the reliance on design systems. A design system is a set of guidelines, reusable elements, and code. Whether used for UI/UX design or for the product's implementation, design systems enhance safety by preventing workers from creating inconsistencies and reinventing things. Using design systems improves all fitness aspects.

Real teamwork

When you designed the way of working (Strategy 1b), one of the choices to make was: when several people do related work, do you want them to operate as workgroups, teams, or Agile teams?

Most likely, the predominant choice was not workgroups, and everyone is now a member of the "project team" or of a "dev team" or "Scrum team." They attend process meetings together and work off a single plan. If working in an office, they might sit in the same space.

However, in many systems (even at Level 3) those are, in fact, workgroups. Work assignments are highly individualized and centrally managed, and the members — who usually specialize in parts of the work — have their own goals and little dependence on others. If they "sprint," it's along parallel tracks. Though they nominally contribute to a shared goal, they don't really share ownership of it or have mutual commitments in the way teams do. If you think critically about your teams, are you seeing signs of that?

Many reasons can explain why those "teams" are not really teams. A common root-cause is that when the system was still at Level 1 or 2, it didn't have the capacity to form teams. Everybody was busy just getting the basics in place — portfolio management, structure and workflow, responsibilities and decision-making, stability. It may not have been safe enough for staff members to engage in real teamwork or for leaders to spend some of their effort on it.

If the above has made you wonder whether a specific team in your system is really a team — as opposed to a group of individuals doing related work — try the following thought exercise. It assumes the team uses Scrum, but if that's not the case, translate the process and roles to your setup.

Imagine that all team meetings went away. Instead, members send the Product Owner (PO) their individual questions and estimates about backlog items. The PO and the Scrum Master (SM) determine the sprint plan, assign tasks, and answer questions all in the backlog management software. Instead of a daily Scrum (standup) and a sprint retrospective, members send their input to the SM, who then distributes a summary and action items. The PO/SM give demos to stakeholders and subsequently update the backlog.

Now ask yourself: Would this *significantly compromise* the outcomes that the team's work produces?

If your honest answer is "no," you have a workgroup, not a team.

This isn't merely a matter of using correct terms. If real teamwork is, in fact, necessary for high system fitness, having workgroups instead will mean falling short on all aspects of fitness. That's because teams approach their work differently.

Teams focus on a mission: creating great products/ solutions that make a meaningful difference. By contrast, groups tend to focus on individual output, which may not combine to create the best whole. In a team, members feel committed to each other, so they lift others up or catch teammates if they fall, which creates resilience and adaptability. Teams have a wider array of options for dividing and managing work and dependencies, so they incur shorter process delays and are likelier to succeed when facing tight constraints or a close deadline. Real teamwork has many personal benefits for the people who experience it, which results in greater engagement and often amplifies the above effects. **The more teamwork takes place in the system, the freer the managers are to manage the system.**

SUPPLEMENTARY RESOURCE: Download the "Workgroup, Team, or Agile Team?" summary from the book's companion website, DeliverBetterResultsBook.com.

With your improvement partners, create a picture of the kind of teamwork that would best fit your system. Clarify the gaps between that picture and your current reality, and analyze their root causes. You might discover a simple reason for gaps: the particular assignment of individuals to teams is not optimal for teamwork. Perhaps some folks don't get along with specific colleagues or are not interested in their team's mission. Some coaching might resolve the problem, or not; you might have to go as far as re-forming some teams (that would be an example of continuing to apply Strategy 1b).

There is another common explanation for the gaps. For teamwork to emerge, folks need to hold three beliefs:

- The team may be smarter and more productive than the sum of its members.

- The team may make smarter decisions than its manager/leader.
- Individuals will make mistakes; supervision isn't the best way to mitigate that.

Your analysis might reveal disagreement or misalignment, among leaders and individual contributors alike, about these beliefs. In this case, you'll need to have some frank conversations — about expertise, trust, and responsibility — before proceeding.

This brings us to the third common explanation. Everyone does hold these beliefs, and leaders have tried to encourage teamwork. However, it's all been tactical, implemented by forming cross-functional teams that have frequent touchpoints in which they plan, review, and improve together. What's missing here, if you recall the mindset model from Chapter 2, is the connective tissue between beliefs and tactics: principles. These principles tell team members and leaders *how to engage* with each other, both during team touchpoints and outside of them. While the principles vary by operating model, they include at least psychological safety, trust, and respect. If you've chosen to have an Agile environment, for instance, there is also transparency, self-organization, collaboration, and consensus.

These interpersonal principles may not be part of the prevailing mindset because fostering them hasn't been anyone's responsibility. They — and the cultivation of teamwork in general — are in leadership's blind spot. The hierarchy largely deals with individuals, which it might even regard as "resources" (physical-world resources don't form teams). To address this, make the growing of a great team that lives by these principles someone's explicit responsibility, or create a role specifically for it. This is particularly critical — and requires time and presence — when a team is still in the forming or storming stage. If there are multiple teams, their leaders ought to collaborate with each on creating and enabling a coherent model of teamwork across the system.

Even with intent, alignment, and clear team leadership, efforts to create teamwork will succeed only to the extent that the system doesn't undermine it. Look closely at your system and see where it *actively discourages* teamwork. The usual suspects include moving people around frequently, setting individual work goals, and conducting output-minded performance reviews. The system might also *subtly discourage* teamwork; the usual suspects there are: how work gets divided among people, what gets measured, and what gets rewarded. In almost all cases, system leaders have the authority to change these around. In others, notably HR-related matters, you'll need to partner with colleagues outside the system.

Collaboration

The third component of this strategy is to increase collaboration, both within teams and across parts of the system.

You probably hear the word "collaboration" a lot. Sometimes though, what people really mean is "cooperation," and they don't realize how different these concepts are.

Collaboration means working together on a task and sharing responsibility for the outcome. The process may take various forms and the work doesn't have to be divided equally, but everyone operates with a stance of shared ownership. In cooperation, on the other hand, people's ownership extends only to their part — what's "on their plate." The system can't force people to collaborate (because that's voluntary) but it can force them to cooperate.

Collaboration and teamwork are also different concepts. While collaboration contributes to the system's fitness for purpose in much the same way that teamwork does, it's more powerful: it's a great way to mitigate the risk of employing human beings, who don't always perform the best when working on their own.

Having said that, your system needs a mix of collaboration, cooperation, and solo work. People's abilities, and the needs of the system both now and in the future, suggest a theoretically ideal mix. In reality, the personalities involved and their need to feel pride, accomplishment, recognition, and self-worth will change that somewhat. For example, I was once a member of a software and content team that officially valued pairing (collaboration among pairs of members). Two members resisted pairing with others and worked almost entirely on their own; they gravitated to parts of the content where that made sense. The rest of us paired up whenever our schedules allowed it.

Increasing collaboration across teams will both help solve problems *and* strengthen the system. It will increase the sideways flow of information that otherwise flows mostly up and down the hierarchy. Cross-wise interactions will reveal common issues and give rise to additional ideas for solutions. Decision-makers, drawing on more real and less filtered information, will make better decisions.

In most value delivery situations I've been in, people were helpful, friendly, and professional. They cooperated. But in almost all of them, they didn't collaborate nearly as much as they could, and not for lack of encouragement, opportunity, or tools: other human and system matters were at play. Based on my observations in various knowledge work situations, I've developed the following model to explain what makes collaboration possible, welcome, and real.

Fulfill prerequisites to collaboration

Before two or more individuals may collaborate willingly on a task — even if they're already colleagues on a real team — *every one of them* subconsciously runs through the following nine prerequisites or "filters" in sequence. If any comes up negative, they won't collaborate. Try this out yourself: before you read on, think of a specific upcoming task on which you might collaborate with others.

1. "Do I have good reasons to work with others on this task?"

Involving more than one person might be necessary for completing the task or a way to improve its results. Other motivations include learning to do better next time, strengthening a relationship, sharing knowledge, and simply having fun.

2. "Do these reasons justify collaboration over cooperation?"

In a way, this is a cost/benefit question. Collaboration may produce better results in a given situation, but it's likely to require greater presence, emotional investment, and energy (all the more so if something goes wrong). Cooperation, which often takes the form of "We'll each do our part, and we'll talk when necessary," makes it easier for everyone to manage their time, energy, and emotional state. A factor that subtly reduces the assumed benefit in the calculation is when folks have distinct roles/titles such as front-end developer, automation tester, business analyst, architect, etc.; it's natural to assume that work would run more efficiently if each person did their own thing.

3. "Can the others make valuable contributions to the task, and will they be there to the end?"

People appreciate collaboration when they perceive that the others contribute *enough* — not necessarily equally — to creating the shared result. The diversity of expertise and knowledge in technology work often leads people to assume it can't possibly happen. In a prime example that I see all the time, back-end developers and front-end developers assume they're too different to collaborate, despite them both being developers. Even if they see the potential, they might assume — based on how work is divided up — that their availabilities wouldn't line up to allow collaboration from start to finish. Flexible hours and hybrid working arrangements, despite their many benefits, present an additional barrier here.

The above three prerequisites are cerebral; you can argue about them logically. However, collaboration is an intense, subjective human experience (whether conducted in-person or online). The next two prerequisites reflect whether the person can afford to collaborate in this instance.

4. "Will collaborating with them be safe for me?"

This question applies to two points in time. While collaborating, can the person afford to be vulnerable — to make mistakes without being chastised, ridiculed, or blamed? And afterward, will the others speak honestly about the person's contribution? On a team I once managed, this was the collaboration-killer for two members. Each one believed that if they worked on something together, the other person would belittle their part to me in our one-on-one meetings.

5. "Will I be treated fairly?"

Folks might feel safe to collaborate with each other, yet worry that the system wouldn't treat them fairly afterwards. This concern is often justified in systems that value individual productivity over team productivity or outputs over outcomes. Think about your environment: does delivery on planned tasks make a better impression than proving that some feature shouldn't be developed at all? In this regard, leaders who give credit to entire teams would do well to also acknowledge — not reward — collaboration and standout contribution, even if they do so in private conversation.

The last four conditions relate to the emotional side of the collaborative experience.

6. "Am I looking forward to the experience of working together?"

Even if the collaboration is safe and fair, will it be enjoyable? Positive, not merely neutral? If these folks have had bad experiences with each other, are they willing to get past them?

7. "Will I be part of creating the experience so that it works for me?"

Some people are introverted, others are extraverted. Some need the physical conditions to be a certain way, others mind them less. Some need frequent short breaks, others can go for hours non-stop. Is everyone willing to co-create the experience and to potentially make some compromises for the sake of working together?

8. "If a conflict arises, will we be able to resolve it?"

Collaboration can go offside and create discomfort. Many people, anticipating this, opt for the safer-feeling alternative of working solo. The greater their self-awareness, emotional intelligence, and empathy, the less likely they are to avoid collaboration.

9. "Will we have rapport?"

Rapport exists between people when they subconsciously send similar visual cues (notably posture, angle of spine, and use of hands) and auditory cues (specifically in tone, pitch, and pauses) that indicate positive engagement in the interaction. Rapport makes an interaction feel human and inviting instead of transactional. People don't need to be friends with their colleagues to collaborate with them, but they do expect to have some rapport when they do that. That is why they sit side by side, or stand together at a whiteboard, or face each other — and why collaboration using online tools doesn't feel as personal and to some, less fulfilling.

People run through this sequence of prerequisites the same way *every time collaboration is an option*, whether that's within their team or with people outside of it. The former case is the common one: a few teammates collaborate on a task that's part of their shared mission. The latter case — when two or more teams, representatives, or managers collaborate to advance a matter that concerns all of them — is probably not a daily occurrence, but no less important.

To increase collaboration, mentally survey the people and their collaboration opportunities, and identify the earliest of the nine prerequisites that's *unmet* for them.

- If it's the same one in most cases, the issue needs a systemic response. For example, at one enterprise product company, everyone assumed that integrating deliverables from specialized team members would produce great features, so they saw no reason to join forces. At an investment firm, it was the third prerequisite that prevented collaboration between IT people and their business counterparts; each "side" thought the other didn't know enough about it to make meaningful contributions in a collaboration (despite having been close colleagues for years). Both cases required conversations among system leaders to change the dynamic.
- If it's a different prerequisite for different people, address it on an individual basis with a good dose of empathy and coaching.

Remove deterrents to collaboration

What if all the prerequisites are met, and people still don't collaborate as much as they could? In this case, see whether any of the following five patterns exists in the system. Each one will deter people from collaborating, and they'll need to proactively decide to go ahead despite it. Some of these deterrents are due to leaders' actions; all of them are on leaders to address.

Work is almost exclusively described by its activities and deliverables. Notice that there are three lenses for viewing work:

- its purpose or intended outcomes, such as a change in user behavior, risk reduction, or validation of a strategy

- the outputs or deliverables that produce those outcomes, such as mockups, features, and steps to reproduce defects
- the inputs or activities that should produce the outputs, such as designing, coding, and testing

Because activities and deliverables are visible and concrete, describing work through these two lenses is easy. However, doing that most of the time may subtly imply that solo work is enough or optimal, that specialization or expertise is critical, or that other needed competencies don't justify collaboration.

Individuals are accountable for results, but teams are not. To the extent that management expects people to perform their specialized tasks, folks will do exactly that. If person A collaborates with person B on moving "their" tasks forward, will that make person A seem less productive, even though that moves the team forward? You'll know this is going on if people use expressions such as "I have a lot on my plate" and "My part is done."

Processes, tools, and metrics imply expectation of individual work. The workflow, the way work gets apportioned, the tools that facilitate both, and what gets measured may give the impression that everything needs to be done solo. Common examples include having daily meetings in which folks answer "What did *I* do yesterday? What will *I* do today?"; using work management software that allows only one person to be an item's assignee or owner; and organizing task boards by team member.

Teams have too much work in process. When there's a lot of work to go through, people assume that parallelizing efforts will maximize the aggregate productivity. That makes it harder to justify collaboration, or to even consider which tasks might end much sooner thanks to collaboration.

Exclusionary behaviors are allowed or tolerated. Behaviors signal openness to collaboration. However, people are often unaware of the signals they send, and that the signals may not convey what they really intend. As a result, some behaviors that are allowed or tolerated discourage others from seeking collaboration. Three common examples are when people are in cliques (they always interact with the same small group), wear headphones most of the day, and use their mother tongue with same-heritage colleagues instead of the team's lingua franca.

If any of these deterrents explains why your people don't collaborate enough, why is it present? If you look closely, you might find that it's accidental, temporary, or otherwise easy to fix. However, you might find that there's a deeper reason: **collaboration isn't valued enough**.

To advance from Fitness Level 1, leadership chose the best few values that would guide the entire way of working. Perhaps collaboration was missing from the set, not implied by it, or not truly implemented. Or maybe, in the months or years since then, a different set of values has taken over. For example, efficiency, predictability, or meeting deadlines might now be overshadowing the collaboration value. You'll see this play out, for instance, if team members usually work "heads down" or wear headphones all day. Look into the matter of intended and de-facto values; it might be time for an adjustment.

Addressing the prerequisites and then the deterrents will make collaboration *possible*. Make it more likely to occur by adjusting processes, crafting working agreements, and upgrading the collaborative aspect of your current meetings. As well, nudge people toward it by creating specific contexts such as communities of practice and hackathons. Remember that no matter how the teams are organized, some cross-team collaboration will always be necessary for system success; make it safe and welcome for people to work across teams as needed.

SUPPLEMENTARY RESOURCE: Download the "How to Make Real Collaboration Possible" handy summary from the book's companion website, DeliverBetterResultsBook.com.

Executing this strategy

Start by making a clear picture of the extent and manifest-ation of contributor safety, real teamwork, and collaboration that would be good for the system. Then use the tests and indicators mentioned earlier to get a clear read on the current situation. Create a plan to close the gap, keeping the following in mind:

- Safety is an enabler for teamwork and collab-oration, but it doesn't have to first be dialed to the max.
- Almost everything in this strategy is a matter of day-to-day behaviors rather than concentrated action.
- Little changes may have a big impact.

> At an investment firm with understaffed IT, a new team of six — all at 50% allocation — found its footing only once management arranged everybody's 50% to overlap. They really became a team a couple of weeks later when one of them pointed to a task on the plan and said, "Why don't we just work on it together and knock it out quickly?" Within two hours of informal "mobbing," the task was done. They marveled at this, saying "If we'd passed it around like we always do, it would have taken us a week!"

This strategy is a necessary enabler for the next two. Your system will be ready for them when people, who would have held back when they had something useful to say, no longer do so; teams that used to act as workgroups now act as real teams; and folks collaborate across the system in many situations that justify it.

This strategy will have "done its part" to move your system to Level 4 when everyone feels both sides of contributor safety and teams enjoy a healthy balance of collaboration, cooperation, and solo work.

STRATEGY 3B: DEFER COMMITMENTS AND INCREASE RELEASE FREQUENCY

Back in Chapter 1, you determined practical and relevant optimums for your system's throughput, outcomes, timeliness, and adaptability. The next strategy will move the system much closer to achieving all of them. To understand it, let's consider two important elements of the operating model — commitments and release frequency.

Systems constantly look ahead to several different horizons or timeframes. The portfolio or roadmap reflect the farthest horizon; in your system, how many years or months do they cover? Projects and releases reflect a closer horizon; how many months long are they, typically? The closest horizon tends to be team-level and a week or two out. Do you have other ones?

Managers and team leaders spend a lot of time planning for those horizons, eventually making various **commitments** and promises based on all that planning. Commitments may be to objectives or goals, to customer and business outcomes, and to solution and execution parameters such as dates, budgets, personnel assignment, requirements, and designs. Take a moment to reflect on the commitments that your system makes for each horizon.

Separately from all this thinking ahead and promising, your system has a **release frequency**: how often it actually delivers something that produces customer or business outcomes. What's the frequency in your case? Calculating it is straightforward if the system works on fixed release timelines. If the time that passes between product releases is variable, what's the average?

Strategy 3b has two interrelated components:

1. Commit to less and plan in less detail for the longer horizons.

2. Reduce the size of releases and release more frequently.

As you implement it, you must control two costs:

- the cost of change (the affordability of likely adaptations)

- the cost of process (planning, coordinating, releasing, etc.)

You're still working off the business and product strategy. You're still striving to identify the right problems to solve and the best outcomes to produce. You're also likely to keep looking ahead to the same horizons. What the strategy's first component changes is *what you commit to and plan* for each horizon. For the longer ones, commit only to the objectives and outcomes that are too critical, risky, or costly to push out. Keep everything else in sight so that you don't come back to it when it's too late or too expensive. Defer commitment to solution and execution parameters as much as possible.

Commitments are important for the progress of an organization, which is why yours probably expects and rewards them. A key assumption of this strategy is that at Fitness Level 3, people make too many specific commitments too early. Doing so reduces their ability to respond to changes of mind, circumstance, or understanding (and has additional consequences, if they don't plan right). Deferring commitments won't make anyone less busy or productive; instead, it will keep more options open and reduce unnecessary constraints.

Examples of using this strategy include:

- If you're to deliver a large program two years from now, commit to the vision and key *outcomes*, but not to a full set of detailed requirements. Plan for some intermediate releases — even if their audience is limited or internal, or the value delivered is low — at least to reduce risk and get feedback on your choices.

- If you commit to a year's worth of projects, choose what to include in the first six months and commit to that, treating everything that would have followed as optional. Repeat six months from now.

- If you plan and release three months' worth of work at a time, start planning six or eight weeks at a time and also releasing updates every couple of weeks.

- If you batch multiple unrelated features together, shift to releasing each one when it's ready.

Note the gradual changes in the above examples. Deferring commitments doesn't mean "make no promises," reducing planning doesn't mean "skip planning," and increasing release frequency doesn't mean "continuous delivery." Rather, you're modifying the way of working to commit, plan, and release **less scope more often**.

Deferring commitments

Deferring commitments (while keeping costs in check) has many benefits, all of which enable the system to deliver better results to customers:

- risk reduction
- easier and earlier pivoting (if necessary)
- less potential for wasted work
- higher resilience to big changes
- greater team engagement

While planning and making commitments are distinct activities, they feed each other and are often done around the same time. Make sure that in your system, plans don't implicitly become commitments just because people spent time thinking about them or showed them to leaders. Between the two, the primary thing to reduce or defer is the commitments, because once they're made, changing them has cascading effects throughout the system and company. By committing to less, you'll inevitably spend less time planning.

Earlier, we looked at three common horizons for planning and commitments: portfolio, project/release, and every week or two. Many companies have an additional one that affects the system: the year. Often related to budgeting cycles, annual planning may force senior leaders to make more commitments than is ideal.

> *VP Engineering at a product company in the education space:*
>
> *"At the start of every school year, we prepare our roadmap for the next 12 months. Between Sales' expectations, our loudest customers, and product enhancements, the roadmaps fill up. They are doable, but there's no room for error. I've been here eight years, and every year some things pop up and we have to revise the roadmaps."*

Changing this dynamic requires conversations at the executive level and a close look at the reasons for the planning being annual and as elaborate as it is. Some companies are realizing great benefits from adopting more-continuous budgeting and planning methods.[2] I've also known leaders who contributed effectively to budget calculations without constraining themselves too much to what that budget would be spent on.

Increasing release frequency

Your customers and users are the first to benefit from a higher release frequency: instead of waiting a while to accomplish some of their outcomes, they're able to accomplish some of them sooner. They also indirectly benefit from releases that focus on business value, because those improve the system's ability to deliver better products/solutions sooner. Increasing the frequency of releases provides more and earlier opportunities to pivot if necessary, better understanding of the system's actual delivery capacity, and more evidence of progress.

Increasing the release frequency takes careful management. It looks different depending on the current frequency, but generally requires more collaborative planning, strategic feature breakdown, efficient testing that proves the code safe to deploy, upgrades to the deployment pipeline, and lower work management overhead. In other words, some aspects of the way of working truly need to change to enable shorter releases. Much like running is not the same as fast walking, *you won't achieve very short releases by cramming the same process into shorter cycles.*

Of the two components of this strategy, focus first on deferring commitments. That will likely lead to cramming less into releases. In turn, that will motivate people to release product/solution updates more frequently and to gradually build up the processes and tools that support it. Don't start this strategy by investing heavily in building the technical capability to release often. Many companies have discovered they weren't ready to take advantage of that capability because their tendency to make long-term deep commitments was so strong.

Controlling costs

Committing, planning, and releasing less scope more often takes a lot of discipline and collaboration across the system. You'll need to be careful to do so while preventing certain costs from rising.

The first is the **cost of change**: what the system will need to pay later — not only in money — for changes. This cost can hamper company plans, because folks often don't realize that changing direction incurs a higher cost than just that of implementing the new idea. If the originally planned item is midway through development, there's the labor for undoing it (completely or partially); if it's already in production, that cost may be higher and even include loss of clients and damage to reputation. There are additional labor costs: tracking, coordination, communication, documentation, risk management, testing, training, etc. And on top of all this, there's often a hidden human cost: the impact to the morale, trust, and engagement of the people who worked hard on the original.

Deferring commitments and shortening releases is generally good for keeping the cost of change down for an obvious reason: if a change is needed, you might learn about it sooner and need to do less about it. Yet, you can achieve this effect only if you're strategic about what you commit to and include in every release. In other words, don't just plan work based on intended outcome and value, because you run the risk of undoing some of it. Map out what might have to change (by your choice or not) both during the work and after delivery, identify the changes with the highest likelihood and effect, and plan accordingly. While this is an Agile concept, it applies also to teams that do big upfront planning, as they *will* be exposed to some changes.

The second important cost to control is **process cost**: the time people spend using the system's process, such as in planning and coordination. Releasing less scope more often tends to spread it out more evenly, and while that doesn't necessarily increase the cost, people will get that impression (you'll hear, "more meetings?!"). Control the process cost by:

- Making sure that all the meetings are worth having (see Strategy 3c)
- Streamlining your use of planning tools
- Enhancing the testing strategy
- Investing in automation to make releases safer and cheaper

- Enabling teams to handle more of the release lifecycle themselves

If applying this strategy does increase the cost over time, check that its benefits are worth the extra cost.

Executing this strategy

Discuss with your fellow improvement leaders: what type and extent of committing, planning, and releasing would be ideal for the system's fitness for purpose?

Plan to close the gap between that and the current state one order of magnitude at a time, such as from 12 months to 6 months, from 6 months to 3, and from quarterly to a few weeks. Each such change may take even a year or more until the system sustains it.

Closing the gap takes this long, and is best done gradually, because deferring commitments affects other systems in the company and is affected by them. Implementing this change requires greater alignment and partnership with all those systems' leaders, otherwise it would create friction and tension, and risk a reversal. This is true even if your teams already use sprints or flow (meaning that they take on just a few work items at a time). It's the extent of long-horizon commitments and the frequency of actual value delivery that matter to improving system fitness.

> *Head of Engineering at a rapidly growing startup:*
>
> *"Our teams are productive and move fast, which is critical for our growth. However, our Finance people are used to working on an annual cycle with detailed budgeting. As a result, we have to treat everything as a project, which delays our getting started, makes iterative development less welcome, and causes our business people to wait long."*

This strategy — especially the part about commitments — often produces varied "can't" and "shouldn't" resistance from system leaders, stakeholders, and executives. If you experience that when broaching the topic, don't counter the resistance head-on. Instead, seek to understand the worldviews or beliefs underlying the resistance. For example, do they believe that technology development professionals ought to be able to make viable, detailed commitments for months ahead? That product releases are an all-or-nothing proposition, so they should include everything? That small releases don't leave time for proper quality assurance? Knowing this will enable you to choose effective responses.

As you defer more commitments and increase release frequency, remember to keep the system stable (Strategy 2b). As mentioned earlier, stability looks different depending on planning cycles and release lengths, but the principles and techniques to achieve it are largely the same.

This strategy will have "done its part" to attain Level 4 once the system is consistently able to focus its attention on new opportunities and changing needs soon after learning about them.

STRATEGY 3C: ENGAGE TEAMS IN PLANNING

The previous strategy dealt with the commitments your system makes. Now, let's focus our attention on **planning**: all the activities that lead to commitments, what they encompass, and how the system will act on them. Common examples of such activities include product discovery, solution design, release and sprint planning, scheduling, and planning migrations.

The next strategy is straightforward: have the relevant teams and experts contribute to each planning activity as meaningfully, collaboratively, and efficiently as possible. Even though these folks may not have more decision-making rights than before — that's a Level 4 strategy — their greater participation can materially improve the planning output. As a result of this strategy, the system may:

- produce better outcomes
- achieve higher throughput by reducing unnecessary work
- deliver more-timely results by reducing delays
- respond better to events

A scientific instruments company was ready to start developing a new instrument. The decision-makers all thought of it as a hardware project with a bit of programming. They put in place teams and plans, and organized an off-site to kick off the project and plan the first release. Acting on advice from the external facilitator, they invited some "related" people, too.

It was thanks to those folks, such as the instrument servicing lead and a researcher, that a few hours into the session everyone had a realization: this was in fact an 18-month *software* project with some firmware and hardware. A smaller but highly cross-functional workgroup went back to the drawing board, and a few months later, relaunched the project.

For staff, contributing their thoughts and expertise at impactful planning junctures — and having them influence choices — increases motivation and all-round engagement. They learn more about the product and understand its context better. Therefore, this strategy also makes the system more adaptable and resilient.

When and how do those teams contribute to planning? Some of that happens asynchronously, usually by commenting on planning drafts and providing data. However, by far the most-used mechanism for conducting planning activities is the meeting. Since your system is at Level 3, it's fair to assume that certain individuals and teams *already* provide input in some planning meetings — but their contributions don't significantly affect planning content and decisions.

A ubiquitous example of this dynamic goes as follows. A team attends sprint planning. The product owner (PO) presents the sprint goal and user stories to the team. Almost all discussions and Q&A, such as there are, take place between the PO and the tech lead or manager. The team's participation amounts to estimating engineering tasks, which they could do without needing a meeting.

The system needs to have moved past Fitness Levels 1 and 2 before you can turn this dynamic around. That's because at those levels, systems leaders are often too concerned about "making ends meet," so to speak, that they don't seek teams' inputs enough or use it effectively.

Better meetings

This strategy doesn't imply having more, longer, or bigger meetings, but it does imply having *better* ones. Making a meeting worth having is mostly a matter of *preparation*. The following method produces good meeting plans but doesn't take long:

1. Determine the meeting's **purpose**. It should be to achieve a meaningful and compelling outcome worth gathering people for. It helps to identify both a rational purpose and an experiential one (how the group will be different as a result of the meeting).

2. Determine the meeting's **deliverables** (its output).

3. Choose the right **people** for it. Every attendee should be contributing and/or learning, and should know exactly why they're there. Decide if declining the meeting invitation is an option and how the meeting would proceed if attendance is partial.

4. Clarify who makes **decisions** and how. The purpose of the meeting might call for team consensus,

leader decision with or without buy-in, or some other method. To the extent that participants make decisions, be clear about what happens if management doesn't like their choices.

5. Craft the **agenda** as a series of open questions that the attendees work through to produce their deliverables. This style of agenda gets people thinking and talking much more than a dry list of topics. When you invite the attendees, informing them of the agenda questions in addition to the meeting's purpose and deliverables will likely prompt initial thoughts.

6. For each question, plan a time-boxed **activity** that has the participants answer the question. The activity can be as simple as talking, working in silence and then combining ideas, or discussing in small groups and then comparing notes.

The agenda and activities should make enough room for **divergence** of contribution and exploration before converging on a deliverable. This built-in slack is critical for collaboration to work its magic; *it's not an inefficiency to cut.* For example, if you're meeting to discover the causes of an incident, the participants can each create a map that reflects their understanding of the causal chain leading up to the incident. They can then discuss the insights that their maps reveal and possibly come up with a better map together.

SUPPLEMENTARY RESOURCE: Download "Examples of Formulating Meeting Agendas as Questions" from the book's companion website, DeliverBetterResultsBook.com.

As you conduct your preparation, take psychological safety into consideration. What would make participants feel safe to participate, to minimally filter their contribution, and to willingly sign up for action items? What could reduce their safety? For example, if you invite more people than necessary — especially senior ones — some participants may be less inclined to speak, or take on certain action items to avoid looking bad. Do you need to have a talk with someone before they attend?

During the meeting, you'll mostly need to work through the plan, but be prepared to adjust it somewhat based on actual discussion. I recommend that you or someone else capture contributions visibly; this simple act enriches the conversation, facilitates idea generation, demonstrates that all voices matter, and increases follow-through. Plan to end the meeting a couple of minutes sooner and then conduct a brief retrospective *about the meeting itself* so you can make the next ones better.

The above tips are written as suggestions to an individual because it's usually effective and efficient, even in a team that works well together, to have a single person (sometimes two) *facilitate* the meeting. The facilitator looks after the process of the meeting so the participants have the best chance of achieving its purpose, for example by making space for people to talk who might otherwise feel unable to get their words in. Different people may take on the *role* of facilitator in different meetings. You'll give your system's fitness a great boost by getting leaders trained in meeting facilitation; it's a relatively small investment and they'll have plenty of opportunities for real-world practice.

> One company put all of its managers, product people, and team leads through a two-day basic training in meeting facilitation. Within a few short months, "meeting" was no longer a bad word. The transformation was palpable, considering that team members had previously always brought open laptops to the meetings, expecting to do "real" work while meetings went on.

Costs of engagement

A meeting, as an event, has a cost. And, it is higher than it might appear on the surface:

- The greater the number of participants, the more work it takes to prepare and operate the collaborative process and its artifacts.

- While their engagement expands the discussion, some of it may lead to pursuing overcomplicated or impractical ideas.

- Folks spend time getting to the meeting and back. They also incur context-switching costs: the time they need to get present, and to later resume the task they left.

- The farther out the meeting is scheduled (to enable optimal attendance), the longer the delay to implementation of its decisions.

Theoretically, you can shorten a meeting by asking people to review material, think, and contribute ideas when they have time prior to the meeting (asynchronously). I say "theoretically" because folks' other priorities usually get in the way.

Nowadays, replacing meeting in person with an online event using collaboration tools can further reduce some of the above costs. It certainly cuts travel time. If participants join for only a part of the meeting, they can use the freed-up time more efficiently.

However, all this cost-cutting may greatly compromise the outcomes. People's ideas don't build well on others' when they arrive in a sequence of disjointed inputs (especially if they are textual, not verbal). Diversity of thought and opportunities for rich exploration are much lower. It's much harder to spark effective self-organization and positive experiential effects such as a feeling of belonging.

Overcoming all these issues requires different and harder work from the facilitator. Be aware of the trade-offs.

Executing this strategy

Make a list of the system's planning activities. Most will be cyclical and immediately apparent from the process; others will be one-offs or merely infrequent. For each one, write down its intended outcomes and then think critically about its *actual* outcomes. Which ones have the biggest gaps?

Start closing each gap by considering who currently contributes to that activity. For best results, who *should* contribute to it? How and when should they engage with each other? You might discover the need to eliminate some meetings, upgrade others, and introduce new ones. Use the preparation tips listed above.

As you make these changes, Strategy 3a should be enough in play that everyone feels safe to give impactful input, both individually and in a team or cross-team discussion. To help each activity's *decision-makers* feel safe about each change, frame it as an experiment. That will help increase buy-in and overcome skepticism, and buy you time for iterating on each new format a couple of times (you won't get all of them right on the first go).

If a meeting seems promising but its outcome is so-so, the meeting might be too short. A few of my clients that used to hate meetings discovered that once they facilitated them better and started seeing benefits, the teams proactively chose to make them longer in order to spark better discussions.

You might find that even after iterating a couple of times on a meeting's format, the level of contribution doesn't justify its cost. Perhaps you can get better results by replacing it with asynchronous collaboration and requests for comments. However, "safe but silent" can have another explanation: it may be the best course of action *from the participants' point of view*. They do have suggestions or ideas, but prefer to not bring them up.

How come? The following possible reasons might sound harsh, but are often real.

- Their influence on decisions is minuscule. Decisions are made almost entirely by other people (product managers, architects, directors, executives) and outside the meetings.

- They don't *have* to say anything. They've learned that the leader/manager is uncomfortable with the silence — and has the accountability anyway — that they'll eventually do the talking and deciding.

- There's little benefit to them. The product's success rests on the shoulders of other people; no team member would single-handedly affect it.

- Silence shortens meetings. Some deadline is coming up, and they'd rather get back to work sooner.

The common thread here: it's a people matter, not a process matter. Discover which of these reasons apply, and work on the primary one — likely outside the meeting room. You might need to go back to Strategy 3a.

This strategy will have "done its part" to move your system to Level 4 once the expanded team engagement in planning clearly leads to better outcomes and is worth the cost.

 SUPPLEMENTARY RESOURCES: Go to DeliverBetterResultsBook.com and download "Workgroup, Team, or Agile Team?," "How to Make Real Collaboration Possible," and "Examples of Formulating Meeting Agendas as Questions."

CHAPTER 8
PROGRESSING FROM LEVEL 4 TO 5

Your system is *in good shape*. It delivers good results: the portfolio is managed well, the way of working is appropriate, and decisions incorporate diverse inputs. The system is also healthy: psychological safety and teamwork are good, boundaries and decision-making are clear, the employees like the culture, and managers have an easy time attracting new talent. Getting here took a lot of work, and leadership's investment in the system is palpable.

At this point, there's still room for improvement — and a certain risk to address. The system runs well when the work is "normal"; however, it takes longer to achieve major outcomes than the company needs it to, for example supporting new customer journeys, upgrading infrastructure, or integrating an acquisition. If work on such outcomes drags on, stakeholders might lose trust and management might lose patience, possibly triggering a breakdown of process and good habits. The time to mitigate this risk is now.

> *"Our Technology department (35 people) is at Level 4. Anything they do on our existing desktop product is fantastic. Now that we need to move to the cloud, they spend a very long time on that* and *struggle to conceive of new and innovative features; they're too used to the desktop version."*
>
> — *D. A., Director of Software Engineering*

Three strategies will now level up the system by increasing performance and mitigating the major-outcome risk. The first is to expand teams' ownership of major outcomes, the second is to improve decision-making, and the third is to reduce the technical cost of change.

STRATEGY 4A: EXPAND TEAM OWNERSHIP

As your system's fitness increased through the lower levels, individuals and entire teams experienced growing ownership. However, even now, their ownership likely extends only to low-impact decisions, such as fleshing out design details and self-organizing around tasks. It's a different story with high-impact decisions such as what outcomes to pursue, using what solutions, with what designs, by what team, using what process. While individuals and teams provide substantial input to such decisions as a result of implementing Strategy 3c (engage teams in planning), making them is still in the hands of a few key people. And that's risky business.

One risk arises when the decision-makers are not the implementers. They may not fully understand the technical intricacies, implications, and complications of their decisions. As a result, they might over-commit, over-simplify, or otherwise create problems across the system.

Paradoxically, asking folks for their input creates another risk. If a decision deviates significantly from the input given and is not accompanied by understandable and defensible reasoning, that's a recipe for fostering disenchantment and mistrust. Furthermore, when the work is over, if the decision's actual outcomes turn out to be problematic, this may lead to further erosion of trust, to apathy, even to anger. All of these would impact the system's fitness.

These risks are real because team members are not emotionless "resources." They are creative people who want to make a difference. Product managers want their products to create the best value for users and the business, designers want to create delightful experiences, and developers want their solutions to be technically sound.

Strategy 4a is to expand teams' ownership of major outcomes — both *defining them* and deciding *how to achieve them.* In other words, to widen their decision-making and responsibility over both product and system matters:

1. Product matters: the outcomes (problems, opportunities, needs, and goals) that the product addresses; the solutions it offers to that effect; the technological capabilities that enable the solutions.

2. System matters, such as processes, execution choices, and task assignments.

This strategy produces several benefits, some of which amplify each other in a virtuous cycle:

- People's motivation and engagement are higher, and they take greater responsibility.

- They're likely to consider more options and to produce more desirable and higher quality outcomes.

- They might make decisions faster than if those decisions had to wait for busy managers.

- Cohesion across the system grows as more people work with each other because of shared interest, not because managers orchestrate it.

- Voluntary turnover is likely lower, which helps retain the culture and the fitness level.

To be clear, the strategy's target is not 100% autonomy, even if everyone wanted to have it all the time (which is rarely ever the case). Based on your context, some product matters should remain the responsibility of certain people for business-related reasons. As for system matters, some level of centralization and cross-system consistency is beneficial. Be careful not to limit people's involvement and empowerment because it feels like an *inefficient use of their time*; make sure you assess the trade-offs carefully.

Examples of greater ownership of product matters:

- Folks break down big initiatives and strategies into intermediate milestones and outcomes. In the workshop depicted below, 14 people from across a company — ranging from team leads to the CEO — met to create the product roadmap for the following nine months. Every opinion counted at face value despite the differences in authority. Prior to reaching Fitness Level 4, roadmapping had been the responsibility of only a couple of people.

The brainstorming portion of the roadmapping workshop

- Teams have time to pursue things that align with the company's mission but are not in the project portfolio, roadmap, or product backlog. A form of this is "20% time": teams get one day every week to explore or study matters of their choosing. Hackathons are another popular form. At one company, the entire digital products department takes two weeks every year for a scheduled "innovation sprint"; anyone can propose ideas, and temporary teams — comprising product managers, designers, developers, and testers — form around the ideas of highest interest to their members.

- Technical teams lead the charge on platform upgrades. At a company in the 3D visualization space, the product is built atop a powerful third-party engine. Moving to new engine versions brings new capabilities and improvements as well as potential feature duplication and code compatibility issues. Product and marketing leaders identify the next version to move to; team leads and QA experts decide together how and when to approach the upgrade.

Examples of greater ownership of system matters:

- If some common needs don't get enough attention because of the way teams' responsibilities are structured, people from anywhere in the system can form temporary task forces and long-term *guilds* to address them. While these structural shifts might be suggested by management, and usually need their blessing (since they represent a change in effort allocation), their composition and operation may be the responsibility of their members.

A *guild* works on a shared need, such as creating reusable UI components and tooling for performance measurement. Unlike traditional functional teams, which have fixed membership and exclusive ownership of their function's work (e.g., "the front-end team"), guild members rotate frequently and work only on matters that don't belong (or don't get attention) in the backlogs of feature teams. Creating guilds in a cross-functional team structure increases diversity of contribution, exchange of ideas, and a sense of shared ownership.

- If the team structure is no longer effective for the system's needs, teams may self-select (reorganize themselves) instead of management designing and dictating the new structure. Self-selection events require careful planning, boundary-setting, and facilitation; done well, they send a strong message of trust and ownership that strengthens the culture.

- Teams may alter their way of working in more ways than they did when fitness was lower. They should still adhere to the system's values and principles, but may have only a few additional boundaries, such as: work with co-dependent teams for shared success; collaborate on any risky work; if you eliminate certain meetings, have viable alternatives; justify your process choices with data. Within such boundaries, for example, a team may replace sprints with flow, experiment with ensemble ("mob") programming as a replacement for individual task assignment and ownership, and redefine their code review procedures — all without asking for permission.

A company needed to make room in the office for a 50% growth in staff, and the impending desk changes made a lot of people nervous. However, with the system already at Level 4 and abiding by a solid people-first ethos, management didn't take a traditional top-down approach to the office redesign.

The director who led the effort asked every team to elect a representative. Together with the designers that the company had hired, he met with all the representatives regularly. Everyone had an equal voice from early discussions to eventually placing their teams on the redesigned floor. Every team was happy with the result and with the process.

The human side of ownership

While this strategy might sound similar to Strategy 3c (engage teams in planning), it goes further by shifting ownership and responsibility. This shift doesn't have to be deep before certain managers start feeling awkward, uncomfortable, or threatened, especially if they believe that their superiors' expectations of them remain unchanged. Therefore, this strategy requires senior management to give their full and unequivocal support, and possibly make some organizational changes.

With more people having greater ownership, the consequences of misunderstanding and misalignment are higher. Leadership mitigates this risk by ensuring extreme clarity of and alignment to the vision, mission, strategy, and values. Another risk is that teams making some choices in isolation might produce discrepancies that impact customers. Leadership mitigates that risk by setting up guardrails, such as expectations about consistency of deliverables, components, and methods. As mentioned in Chapter 3, people must know their boundaries if their ownership is to be real and effective.

The teams we're talking about already have *contributor safety,* which was cultivated in Level 3: they're comfortable engaging where others are involved and can do their jobs without fear of failure or trouble. Increased ownership requires a higher standard: *challenger safety,* which is the ability to challenge choices and the status quo. Some ways to make challenger safety real include:

- Adapt the system's metrics and rewards to prevent it from inadvertently punishing experimentation and reasonable risk-taking.

- When people propose new ideas outside of their areas of responsibility, give those ideas a fair shake.

- Coach people to debate issues and to accept feedback on professional grounds without taking it personally.

- Allow reopening of discussions if new information comes to light.

- Help managers engage in meetings in ways that don't unintentionally suppress others' contributions.

In terms of the behaviors and attitudes needed from leadership (at all levels), many of the suggestions presented in Chapter 3 apply here. Of particular note is leadership's *trust* that people have the competence to make effective choices and carry them out well. If people lack that competence, leadership should help them develop it. And when they have it, leadership makes their trust visible and real by replacing control with steering and guardrails, removing impediments to decision-making, and supporting people when they experience hesitation, misalignment, and setbacks. As a consequence of all this, don't start executing this strategy until both the teams and leadership are ready for it.

Executing this strategy

Start by making an inventory of impactful product and system matters that folks deal with on a regular (though possibly infrequent) basis. As mentioned earlier, this may include both defining outcomes, such as increasing innovation and system resilience, and deciding how to achieve them, such as experimenting with promising new features and reducing technical debt. Then add to the list other major matters that are being considered or are about to kick off. Examples of such work from recent clients include streamlining the UI for common use cases, testing a novel approach to detecting fraud, and expanding the product to address a new vertical.

For each of these items, note briefly who owns it and who only provides input. Note also the outcomes that the recurring ones have produced and that the other ones are supposed to produce. Then ask yourself, where might increasing certain teams' ownership achieve better outcomes and be worth it? Pick one or two of these areas that are strategic and valuable but not extremely risky, and design an experiment. Starting to execute this strategy with an experiment (or several) will teach everyone a lot without creating hard-to-reverse changes in the distribution of power and responsibilities. Remember to use system thinking: try to anticipate the effects of system relationships and loops on the experiment and its results (see Chapter 2).

Every experiment in increasing folks' ownership needs some parameters:

- If a team needs to be assembled, there should be clear criteria for doing so.
- In continuation of Strategy 2a, it should be clear which people make each decision and how.
- Set expectations with people about basing their decisions on evidence and making them traceable.
- They should be accountable to making certain decisions within a reasonable amount of time (but without rushing) and to pivoting when necessary.

Keeping these parameters to a minimum and letting folks figure out the rest will help them feel both safe to act and *trusted* to act.

> A Master Data Management team needed to switch their database infrastructure to another provider. Despite the high priority of this work, it wasn't

> moving fast enough because the team was busy with consumer-facing features.
>
> Management asked the team for ideas, and they suggested that the systems analyst, a senior developer, and the architect would temporarily leave the team to focus on the database switch and migration. This "SWAT team" received management's blessing to do what it took and to make all the decisions; the only stipulation was that they continue to work in the main team's space and participate in the sprint meetings, so they'd remain in the loop and keep sharing their expertise. After six weeks, the SWAT team finished their work and rejoined the main team. This experiment left a good taste, demonstrating the effect of fully trusting the team.

As you choose targets for increased ownership, pragmatism is critical. Not all team members may be interested in shouldering greater responsibility. They may not be ready for it. Also, the scale of the system might present certain limitations; if so, some "descaling," as mentioned in Strategy 1b, may be helpful now.

This strategy will have "done its part" to move your system to Level 5 when teams take major product and system matters from start to finish with minimal pushing, orchestration, or intervention by management.

STRATEGY 4B: IMPROVE DECISION-MAKING

Every day, people in your system make decisions. These decisions produce outcomes. Some of the outcomes affect business results.

For example, say that consumers can access your product's site or app as anonymous visitors or as holders of free accounts. You've made a change: when a visitor creates a free account, they have to provide less information about themselves. That has led to a decrease in drop-offs during account creation, which is both a customer outcome (more people end up having accounts and gaining higher value from the product) and a business outcome (you have more identified users). There can be a cascade of additional effects from these outcomes.

The eight strategies you've implemented so far would have improved the quality of decisions: people focus better thanks to limiting concurrent work (Strategies 1a and 2b), inputs to decisions are richer through increased safety and collaboration (3a), fewer plans are wrong thanks to deferring commitments (3b), and so on.

Everyone means well with their decisions: their *intended* outcomes are all positive. But results are a matter of the *actual* outcomes, which may match the intended ones or not, and which may be positive or not.

> I was visiting a company's website to book two tours for a vacation, when I discovered they had a promotion: 10% off if I booked using their app. Presumably, their intended outcome was to increase app adoption or to increase sales. However, cart management was broken in the app, and customer service declined to offer a comparable coupon for booking on their website. Actual outcomes: lost sale, an upset customer, and a negative review in the app store.

Recognizing (and sometimes anticipating) negative actual outcomes tends to be easier with user-facing decisions. For instance, new product behavior may confuse or worry enough users to cause a flood of calls to customer service. Turning off a feature may frustrate users enough to write negative reviews. Adding new premium functionality and raising the price, or enabling more functionality in the free version, may reduce sales.

Prioritization decisions can result in negative outcomes as well.

"A client reported a problem with a service request form. Under specific conditions, a checkbox was ticked on the backend when it shouldn't have been. On our side, we thought this was trivial and very low priority. When I visited the client, she took me into a room with a TV and said: 'Whenever the box is ticked, that TV reports an urgent issue and we must dispatch a team of experts to deal with it. Anytime it's incorrectly ticked, it costs us at least $100K.' Once we became aware of the cost of that simple checkbox problem, we deployed a fix within a few days."

— Dave Jacques

With decisions that affect the system or the making of the product/solution, negative outcomes may take longer to materialize. And, as the following three examples demonstrate, the effects of the decider's call may spread far beyond its nominal scope. It can therefore be harder to trace the impact back to the decisions (and in some cases, easier to blame the doers for problems).

- It's common for engineering departments to develop a "test base class," one that provides common setup and teardown functionality for unit tests. The intended outcome is worthy: make writing tests easier and quicker, and reduce duplication between tests. However, in some companies I've visited, that base class did too much, and most tests didn't need any of its functionality. Immediate negative outcome: adding any test caused the entire suite to run slower. Another negative outcome followed once the suite included a few dozen tests and took several minutes to run: the engineers stopped writing tests altogether.

- A company in the press release management space kicked off a rewrite of its main product, basing it on a scalable six-tier architecture. Within a few months of their Scrum teams starting the rewrite, development slowed to a crawl. A simple task to add a field to some form took a week, because code had to be written and tested for six different tiers. This high cost of change had a secondary outcome: it motivated product and engineering to avoid changes by preparing big specs and designs before coding anything, a Waterfall tactic that they had been trying to move away from.

- In many Agile environments, leaders and teams create an elaborate template for user stories in the backlog management application. They achieve their intended outcome: people put more thought into stories and thereby reduce confusion and rework. However, they tend to produce an undesirable outcome as well: because of the administrative overhead, people push more scope into their stories, and later avoid splitting them into smaller ones — two effects that work against their intended Agility.

Strategy 4b is to improve both the inputs to decisions and the decision-making processes. The endgame is straightforward: have the decisions made in the system *produce more positive outcomes and fewer negative outcomes.*

Improve inputs to decisions

Every decision affects some people, whether directly or indirectly. Start by understanding who they are, what their objectives are, and *what they optimize for* in getting their objectives met.

> Soon after the COVID-19 pandemic began, many supermarket chains adopted online grocery shopping. They all pursued the same fundamental customer objective: getting food without going to the physical supermarket. My family's regular supermarket chain did so by mimicking the in-store experience, using pickers who would text us if anything was missing, which happened often. Due to the recurring letdowns, we switched to (and have stayed with) another chain that optimizes for something different: peace of mind. They offer a smaller selection but we always get what we order.

Thinking about the customers and stakeholders this way is also useful when making decisions about the system. Say you're designing a code review process. The objective is to catch problems early and cheaply, and the customers are fellow developers. What would they like the process to optimize for: catching the most problems, learning from colleagues, minimizing the turnaround time, or perhaps minimizing the headache and overhead of providing reviews? Knowing the answer would help you design the most appropriate process.

You might need to discover more information about the various parties affected by the decision. Sometimes, all it takes is asking the right people the right questions. Other times, you'll benefit from producing an interim deliverable and collecting feedback on it (assuming the feedback is relevant and timely). You might need to run a test, a study, or an experiment on some part of the decision before moving on with the rest. Generally, the more evidence you have for a decision — and the more explicit and honest you are about your confidence level — the likelier you'll be to make better decisions.

Improve the decision-making processes

Decision-making is a process carried out by human beings. Making better decisions, therefore, depends on both process factors and human factors. Let's start with the process ones.

Process factors

Outcome-thinking. Every time you make a decision, you might start thinking about activities and outputs; that's a default human behavior. Instead, first gain clarity on the purpose and outcomes, and then determine suitable activities and outputs. For example, say you've identified the need for a user study, and your go-to for conducting such studies are qualitative interviews. If the study's purpose is to determine whether to pursue a new product direction, and its outcome is a clear yes or no, a simple questionnaire might suffice.

When you think about outcomes, consider both intended ones ("What do we want to have happen?") and actual ones ("What might also happen?"). Naturally, you won't be able to foresee all the actual outcomes, because you operate in a complex system, have limited information, are subject to a host of cognitive biases, and can't see the future. But you can identify many possibilities, and use them to inform your choice. For example, if your user study asked certain open questions, the responses might provide good customer language for marketing, or some respondents might turn into early adopters. Alternatively, the study could tip your hand to the competition, or make a bad impression on the respondents.

Such outcome-thinking is not limited to product management and UX choices. Use it for *every* decision made in the system: leading people, allocating funds, launching initiatives, defining deliverables, determining acceptance criteria, sequencing tasks, designing meetings, and more.

System thinking. Some actual outcomes result from the decision being made within a system. As you contemplate possible actions, consider what might happen as a result of the system's relationships and loops. Again, you won't be able to predict all the effects, but you can definitely think through likely ones.

Take, for instance, a common managerial question: a team is getting big, should I split it into two? Superficially, that may reduce communication overhead and increase productivity. It might also improve teamwork — for example, by separating two teammates who don't get along — and therefore increase productivity even more. However, it might also create dependencies between the two smaller teams, and the resulting delays would reduce throughput. Each of these scenarios would also affect the team members' engagement and motivation, and therefore the ability to manage the teams effectively. If you've been in this situation before, what other effects did you see?

Cost of change. Use various methods to reduce the risks and costs of changing course after the decision is made. Traditional methods for achieving this rely on extensive thinking, analysis, and planning. Other methods, some taken from the Lean and Agile philosophies, include:

- Experimenting and testing on a smaller scale to maximize the learning needed for making the decision

- Explicitly considering the most likely and expensive changes — both while implementing the decision and later — and planning accordingly

- Deferring the decision to the last responsible moment: waiting to make it with the most information while the risks and costs are still acceptable

- "Strong opinions, weakly held": making an imperfect but changeable decision early, and as time allows, iterating on it using disconfirming data

- Generating, and possibly pursuing, multiple options for a given goal

Program manager at a bank:

"Before building a new tool for advisors (price tag: $3m), we wanted to see whether and how a certain technology would integrate with Salesforce. We paid its provider $50K to test it out for us. Within a few weeks, we knew it was feasible and had picked the best technical avenue.

It was also good that we hadn't committed to the full project, because soon after this proof of concept, we realized that other projects had higher priority."

Counter-arguments. A common pitfall in technology development may derail all the above mentioned techniques: falling in love with our ideas. We tend to put a lot of thought into why a feature, strategy, or change is great, and a lot less into why it might not be. Doing that can be really uncomfortable, and sometimes hard or risky if the idea comes from higher-ups (hence the euphemism, "Let's play Devil's advocate for a moment."). Incorporate a step into your decision-making process in which you answer, "Why should we *not* go ahead with our idea?". This step will remind you to ask this question and, with time, get your colleagues used to it.

Evolution. If the decision regards a significant amount of work meant to produce a large outcome, approach it in an evolutionary manner: aim for the most helpful sub-outcome, work on it, learn from the actual outcome, repeat. This approach enables you to make progress while spreading out decision-making and its attendant risks. One good way to do this in product development is to interleave discovery and delivery (and to conduct them cross-functionally) instead of treating them as big distinct phases.

Human factors

To enable your system's people to implement these process factors and methods effectively, put the following human factors in place:

Challenger safety. Making a decision can be a big responsibility. In organizations, it's often accompanied by tension and fear among the deciders, their managers, and the input providers. The suggestions given here may compound the tension, because they invite people to make assumptions about others' behaviors and the subsequent effect on the system and the company. Folks must feel enough challenger safety (as described in Strategy 4a) to use these techniques without being seen as difficult, negative, or defiant.

Thinking in bets. In my experience, managers often feel pressure — whether external or internal, real or imagined — to make decisions with confidence, or at least to appear confident in them. That's unhelpful, because *everyone* makes their decisions with incomplete information supplemented by assumptions and guesses. You can reduce the pressure by borrowing a recent idea from the product world: reframe each decision as a *bet*. This will make explicit the assumptions behind the decision and normalize the tension. For example:

- We'll use the open-source library ABC to increase our productivity. → We're *betting* that over the long term, using ABC would save considerable time and headache compared to developing its functionality ourselves.

- We've prioritized the product backlog. → We're *betting* that our chosen ordering of the backlog would provide the best customer value with minimal rework and migrations.

- We're letting the teams self-select. → We're *betting* that allowing the teams to self-select would yield better teamwork and productivity than if the directors determined team memberships.

Think back to several situations in which you made decisions with certainty and confidence. Also think back to other situations in which you weren't certain about your choice but had to proceed anyway. I expect that in the latter case, you were more likely to reflect later, "how well did that turn out? Would I make the same choice again?" Thinking in terms of bets helps make this reflection habitual.

> *Terminology note:* Besides *bet*, other popular words are *hypothesis* and *prediction*. They are not exactly the same and have different connotations. Choose the most palatable word for the people you work with.

Humility. All decisions rest on assumptions, and folks are always at risk of making decisions with unjustified certainty or unproven assumptions. You can't eliminate that risk, but you can mitigate it by cultivating humility. One technique for that is to inject "how do we know" questions into your interactions with them, such as:

- How do we know that our understanding of the business problem was (and remains) correct?
- ... our intended solution is viable?
- ... people would actually use our solution?
- ... the feedback we've solicited is honest?
- ... we're spending our time well?

Make a habit of asking these questions tactfully, helpfully, and safely. With time, they'll inspire more and more people to regularly check assumptions, notice their biases and blind spots, and validate choices.

Collaboration. Outcome-thinking, system thinking, and the other factors and methods might sound simple, but they take considerable mental effort, and they are limited by people's worldview, information, and biases. That makes them great candidates for collaboration! Moreover, making decisions collaboratively — owning them together — increases safety, since folks don't need to take risks all on their own.

Executing this strategy

There are two "low-hanging fruit" actions you can take right away.

First, look for places in the system's processes where people don't base their decisions enough on outcomes. For an easy start, observe team and management touchpoints. For example, you might find that in sprint planning, folks make decisions about story details, code, defects, impediments, or the next deployment without explicitly basing them on the problems they mean to solve. Or, if you attend the weekly management meeting, you might hear plenty about project status and tracking-to-plan, but little discussion of newfound problems, needs, or opportunities.

In each situation, what are the consequences of operating this way? In the examples above, they might include considerable wasted work and missed opportunities to pivot. Once the consequences are clear, collaborate with the relevant leaders on improving the process.

Second, see if some decisions are affected by the metrics being collected (or more specifically, the consequences attached to those metrics). For example, look at teams' decisions about the work to do next. If they tend to pick easy features over more complex, experimental, or valuable ones, and managers monitor the number of features delivered or team velocity, the metric might be playing a role in the teams' choices. Work with management on changing the metrics or the mindset with which they're used. (See more on the risks of metrics in Strategy 2b.)

Next, make sure people feel enough challenger safety (see Strategies 3a and 4a for guidance on creating safety). Then you can start putting mechanisms in place to observe and analyze the actual outcomes of decisions. Expect to have different mechanisms for product and design decisions, engineering ones, and system leadership ones. You might not be able to *measure* a lot, but even qualitative data can be helpful. For some decisions, review the data regularly, for example in team retrospectives. For other decisions, schedule later review points already at decision-making time.

At this point, you can improve the inputs to decisions, the human factors of effective decision-making, and the process factors in any order. Every little bit helps. Remember, the goal is not perfection; it's to produce more positive outcomes and fewer negative ones.

This strategy will have "done its part" to move the system to Level 5 when both the negative outcomes from decisions and the overall cost of decision-making are acceptable to the company.

STRATEGY 4C: REDUCE THE TECHNICAL COST OF CHANGE

Your system and its product undergo change all the time, and the change costs you.

Some people leave and others join. Teams start using new tools and stop using others. Demands from loud customers result in changes to plans. Aging third-party components need to be replaced. Something a developer slapped together for a customer demo needs to be made production-ready. The list goes on.

By implementing the strategies for Levels 1-3, you've been reducing the *cost of change* by avoiding some unnecessary work in various ways. Managing the project portfolio for outcomes and capacity results in building more of the right and less of the wrong. Rationally designing the way of working has reduced unnecessary flux in team structure and process. Cultivating safety, teamwork, and collaboration has helped avoid some cases where people made bad choices because they didn't talk to anyone (and probably decreased turnover too). Deferring commitments and planning less scope more often has reduced the likelihood of major unwanted changes to the product.

What the previous strategies don't fully address is the *technical* cost of change: how much the system spends on technical modifications to the product.

Three types of such change are due to past choices:

- Some of the product's behaviors stop being relevant, or some of its construction becomes outdated or ill-fitting. The choices made initially were fine and the technical investment was sound, but now you have to modernize them. Common examples include migrating from on-premise to cloud hosting, replacing a third-party platform or upgrading to its current version, and removing outdated business rules.

- In other parts of the product, the original investment was sound but deliberately minimal — just enough to seize opportunities — and after some time, it's no longer enough and you need to pay off this debt. For example, a certain piece of code isn't reusable as-is, but making it fully reusable would save other development costs; or, a component is designed to work well under moderate load conditions, but it now needs to support higher loads.

- Some problematic past choices make it hard to write, test, or fix code, and they can't be ignored any longer. Every software system has these in spades in the form of cut corners, ill-advised designs, and overly complicated code.

These three types of change are not trivial, but they're not a daily occurrence and don't usually require urgent attention. However, there's a fourth type of change that occurs all the time: as part of developers' regular work, they make modifications to the product — even when they add brand new features.

The list of possible modifications is *long*. Here are a few: creating a branch in a use case, enhancing an interface, adding a configuration parameter, replacing texts, breaking up a large function or class, making a piece of code reusable, and upgrading the architecture. For each of them, the team needs to test their work and correct mistakes, find what else needs to change, perform necessary migrations, update documentation, and remove what's no longer necessary. All this occurs both during the initial work and later as part of maintenance and enhancements.

That's how much technical change your system deals with, and it costs time. To the extent the time spent exceeds its ideal minimum, it impacts the system's throughput, timeliness, and adaptability. Since time is money, there's an impact to cost-efficiency too. On the human front, the technical complexity of the product can make the changes unsafe and difficult, so people avoid them ("Don't touch that, you don't know what it's connected to!"). And if that's not enough, the cost of change generally increases as the product grows and the choices made in its construction continue to be less than perfect.

> *"My team had decided to have its client and cloud solution communicate through a specific internet address. The work to determine the URL and set it up was quick. Later, we realized we needed multiple URLs, since not all clients were on the latest version. Making the necessary changes to the client and cloud solution took two weeks."*
>
> — *Software development manager*

Usually, your teams *know* whether the technical cost of change is high; just ask them. You can also easily spot the dynamics that correspond to it. Here are a few examples; do you see any of them in your system?

- Instead of the design evolving to support the business strategy, it grows haphazardly (corresponding to a patchwork of user stories and change requests).

- The product's complexity increases faster than the teams can manage it.
- Developers don't work cleanly enough as they rush to meet deadlines and sprint commitments.
- The teams aren't truly confident that the code would work correctly in production.
- Automated test coverage (even if nominally high) is ineffectual, fragile, or not maintained.

SUPPLEMENTARY RESOURCE: Download "Technical Cost of Change Self-Assessment Questionnaire" from the book's companion website, DeliverBetterResultsBook.com.

Strategy 4c is to keep the technical cost of change affordable. It has two components, which are largely independent:

1. Reduce the cost of the likeliest changes to existing parts of the product.
2. Develop new parts in a way that makes their likeliest changes affordable.

This strategy is an investment in the system's future performance. It's tricky, because you can't tell the future and theoretically any change can occur. One extreme response to this matter is to do only what's needed now, which may be irresponsible; the other extreme is to try to make the product so generic it can deal with any change, which is impractical. Aim for a reasonable, economical, and sustainable balance between these two extremes; that balance is specific to your particular situation.

You might be wondering why this strategy isn't indicated for fitness levels lower than 4. In my experience, systems at Level 1 have no bandwidth or appetite for it; taking care of the basics in the present is more important than preparing for possible futures. Level 2 systems, as mentioned in Chapter 6, do overhaul some gnarly code or automate some tests, but only to the extent it helps stabilize the system and make progress more predictable. Level 3 systems have a paradox: leaders are satisfied with their results, so they give insufficient attention to the risk and cost of future change. At Level 4, the readiness is there, as is the risk of putting this matter off any longer.

Reduce the cost of changing existing parts of the product

In the ideal state, your teams can change any part of the product easily and safely at an acceptable cost. In real life, that won't be the case everywhere and for every kind of change, but it doesn't have to be, and you can be strategic about it. Focus your efforts on parts where expensive change is most likely, and make those parts cheaper, easier, and safer to work with. Tactics for doing that include:

- Decouple entities and components so that a change in one has minimal knock-on effect on another.

- Develop effective and efficient automated tests and checks that verify that expected behaviors (both at the unit level and end-to-end) match intended behaviors. Run them frequently so you can discover and pinpoint breakage quickly.

- Remove unnecessary complexity. Make the design as coherent and simple as possible.

- Automate repetitive activities, especially error-prone ones.

- Write relevant team-facing documentation and keep it current.

Additional tactics for the software portion of your product include:

- Break apart components or objects that do too much into smaller, focused ones.

- Replace idiosyncratic or under-engineered code with intent-revealing code using proven design patterns.

- Refactor code to remove code smells (design *antipatterns* that make code unsafe and hard to work with).

Develop new parts in a way that makes their likeliest changes affordable

Say you're creating a high-level design for some feature or capability. You're already considering users' problems and expectations, technical possibilities and limitations, standards, and non-functional requirements. Also consider: what are the likeliest changes this feature or capability might undergo? That could be to handle increased scale, expose information differently, support additional use cases, and so on. While actually designing for these possible futures might be premature or costly, create a design that can be easily adapted for them if they occur.

> *VP R&D at a cybersecurity company:*
>
> *"Ten years ago, our product handled one million events per day. Planning for massive growth, we established a "10x exercise": every six months, we'd review the architecture for faults and limitations, and then enhance it to support 10 times the current load. By doing this regularly, we've now scaled to hundreds of billions of events per day, and never had any catastrophic outages or failures."*

As for day-to-day development work, say you're a team member picking up a new work item. It's part of a bigger portfolio item and should take a few days to complete. Ideally, its purpose is clear, and you know what achieving it successfully looks like (what your team might call "acceptance criteria").

Between now and when the task is done, you'll choose a sequence of steps to take. Each step also involves making choices, such as how to use certain technical elements, which data to pass where, or which design pattern to use. Implement Strategy 4c by basing some of your choices on likely expensive changes occurring during the work and after it's done, whether due to new discoveries, technical complications, or feedback from others. Though this idea is an element of the Agile mindset, it's relevant also for systems that front-load the thinking and deciding, because they will get some things wrong and experience some changes. It's a habit; incorporate it into your system's way of working.

> For an example of doing this with a development activity — albeit not of code — consider my process for writing my weekly advice newsletter, the 3P Vantage Point (3PVantage.com/newsletter/). Once I'm clear about the message that I want to convey, I choose the piece's tone and main elements, including examples and stories. I draft most of the text loosely and ask my wife (who's also my business partner): do you understand what I'm trying to say here? What do you think about the length, tone, and flow? Based on her feedback, I might flesh out the text or change it around considerably. She reads it again; there are usually no more major changes at this point, just wording and grammar. When I've finalized the text, we collaborate on writing the headline and optionally adding a visual. This

> process almost eliminates the risk of requiring major rewrites, and the entire writing activity takes an acceptable amount of time.

Working this way imparts technical agility: the ability to gracefully and economically adapt both your work and your product to relevant change. If such change materializes, it's less likely to throw you off or blow your timeline.

Following is a set of technical agility principles, some of which your system might already be applying to large-scale work. Now, help teams regularly apply them when carrying out small-scale technical work. Reinforcing each other, these principles reduce the *scope*, and thereby the *cost*, of change that might be needed during work and after the work ends.

Evolutionary design. Produce deliverables iteratively and incrementally. This principle was suggested in Strategy 2b (stabilize the system) in regard to portfolio items; it also applies for the smaller-scale work items. This principle helps keep your product in a working state, even though some functionality may be partial. An example of a tactic that implements it is test-driven development: achieve the intended product behavior one micro-behavior at a time by working in small test-code-refactor cycles.

Rapid feedback. Learn and make informed decisions quickly and frequently. At this point, the system probably has multiple feedback loops involving users, customers, business partners, and peers; supplement them with even faster feedback loops, for instance using automated checks (assuming they're fast, reliable, and robust) or by working in pairs/ensembles.

Small, safe steps. Proceed in tiny steps that are easy to test and undo. This principle takes the ideas of breaking work down, making reversible decisions, and getting rapid feedback to a micro level. It allows you to quickly realize what doesn't work and to then change direction. Test-driven development implements this principle too.

One thing at a time. Sequence your tasks; don't start one while doing another. At Level 4, work-in-process limits are probably a familiar concept at the portfolio and team level. At the individual level, though, folks might still be doing too many things at the same time, such as cleaning up some code while investigating a defect, or reviewing a peer's code while working on their own task. Though such multitasking might be helpful in certain situations, the distraction may also increase the chance of making mistakes.

Simplicity. Achieve the intended outcome in the simplest way that will do and that you're not likely to regret quickly. Instead of producing a deliverable so generic it can handle every eventuality, make it *simple* so it's cheap to adapt. And, as you work on a task, be mindful of the complexity of your choices. If you notice yourself introducing unnecessary complexity, remove it before continuing with the task.

Clean work. Ensure the deliverable has high internal integrity, making it easy for others (and you) to work on it later. Instead of defaulting to writing documentation to explain code, prefer to refactor it (make small behavior-preserving transformations) to make it cleaner and more intent-revealing. Truly finish what you start: add necessary tests, remove code smells, remove unused code and branches, and process "TODO" comments. On the rare occasions you have to do quick and dirty work, schedule its cleanup time. By doing all this, you'll minimize later surprises.

Shared responsibility. Be jointly responsible — with the entire team — for everything about the work, acting as if you own it. Hopefully, a lot of that is in place due to Strategies 3a (increase safety, teamwork, and collaboration) and 4a (expand team ownership), but there might be more room for that at the task level. Enable people to contribute outside narrow specialties (see Strategy 2b), even if only by way of advice or review. Create team norms around technical feedback to make it welcome and helpful. Make code reviews smaller and more frequent, and if possible, provide them in conversations instead of in offline commentary. All this will help you avoid getting too attached to, and reluctant to remove, code that harms the design and increases the cost of change.

Executing this strategy

While this strategy might seem relevant only for engineering or development, *making it possible* requires system-wide support. That's because the system's current dynamics push back on it.

The first component — reducing the cost of change in the existing product — doesn't seem to add value in the present, has some risks, and eats into the time available for new development. Though engineering leaders and teams might try various tactics to make it a regular activity, such as dedicating every other Friday to code cleanup or including technical work items in every sprint, in my experience they quickly succumb to the pressure of having to keep delivering new stuff.

To get this component of the strategy off the ground, get engineering leaders *and* product leaders/business partners *and* management together in a room. Help them realize that they have a business problem — of sustainability, quality, and reliability — that is not getting any smaller. Explain what prevents the technical teams, even though it might look like they should be on top of the problem, from dealing with it fast enough. Help the leaders reach a shared decision about this investment in the company's future and how they might implement it sustainably and gradually (a big-bang approach may not be practical).

As with the rest of the work in the system, use portfolio items and work items to capture quality-improvement and other cost-reduction work. Each item should explicitly describe its specific outcome; doing this will also allow non-developers to understand it and its relative importance. Some of those outcomes may be particularly valuable in the short term by enabling upcoming development, so sequence the items accordingly.

The second component — doing new work with the cost of change in mind — may also save development costs in the short term, and still, most systems push back against it. Here is how: product owners/managers want to enhance product features; the system-wide expectation to show consistent throughput ("velocity") focuses folks on short-term outputs over long-term outcomes; and the technical people who understand the risk struggle to make an effective case for its mitigation. Throw in the short tenure most people have in their roles these days, and one's low technical agility today becomes somebody else's cost of change problem tomorrow.

What this means is that if technical agility is lower than it needs to be, you probably won't increase it much by training your developers, hiring more experienced ones, or holding them accountable for it. You have to start by looking for the fundamental causes in the system that prevent technical agility from being higher.

Chances are, some of those causes have to do with the relationship between the three parties mentioned above: development, product/business, and management. There are unvoiced assumptions, unreal expectations, and unaddressed tensions. In such a case, help the three parties to make an intentional, explicit, and mutual commitment to establishing and maintaining high technical agility. Next, make the commitment actionable with strategies and tactics. For instance:

- Expand planning conversations to consider likely future changes and the cost associated with making them.

- Notice when you need to make assumptions about the product's future, and make them collaboratively.

- Train the developers on technical agility skills and practices (most developers haven't had occasion to learn them).

- Cultivate enough challenger safety (Yes, that's in every Level 4 strategy!) so they can flag unsafe and costly code that they encounter while doing new work.

- Be strategic about taking on technical debt and actually pay it off early.

- Include an expectation of code cleanliness in your code review checklist or definition of "done."

The two components of this strategy are independent, and any little bit helps. If starting both feels like too much change, focus on the first component. As the teams get used to cleaning up high-cost-of-change code, they'll be more conscious about not creating it in the first place.

Common to both components is the cross-system, intentional commitment to keeping the cost of change affordable. You're making that investment in a judicious manner based on the information you have now, expecting to make it back later. It's how today's work remains an asset and doesn't become a hidden liability.

This strategy will have "done its part" to attain Level 5 when the system is consistently able to properly implement reasonable changes to the product in a reasonable amount of time.

SUPPLEMENTARY RESOURCE: Go to DeliverBetterResultsBook.com and download "Technical Cost of Change Self-Assessment Questionnaire."

CONCLUSION

Improving value delivery takes time and effort, leadership and partnership, determination and patience, vision and pragmatism.

And then there's the question of *how* to do it. Given your current situation, what changes will effectively and efficiently lead to delivering better results?

SQUARE, the model I've presented in this book, provides high-level answers based on many years of consulting work, observation, and study. It rests on several premises:

- The target of improvement is a *system*. This construct is bigger than a team or a function, and smaller than the company.

- The goal is to make the system fit for its purpose. That's relative and contextual; copy-pasting how others have achieved fitness is not a winning strategy.

- Holistic improvements yield better results than isolated improvements.

- A specific set of incremental improvements can be more welcome, effective, and sustainable than big-bang transformation.

- Implementing too many changes at the same time, even if they're all seen as net positive, can overwhelm people and be self-defeating.

- Change starts with people, not process.

Every organization cares about the productivity and fitness for purpose of its value delivery, though these matters manifest differently. Therefore, SQUARE's strategies may play out differently in your organization than in others.

Remember to not go at it alone. Work with your superiors, peers, and other colleagues who want or need to deliver better results. Show them the book and use it together as your guide to unlocking your organization's potential.

For next steps:

1. Review the leadership foundation described in Chapters 2 and 3, and determine what you need to put in place before acting on SQUARE's strategies.

2. If you haven't yet, perform the fitness assessment from Chapter 1.

3. Study how your system has been applying the lower-level strategies. Address significant gaps (Level 1 gaps first, then Level 2 gaps, etc.)

4. Use Chapter 4's guidance to decide how and when to approach your current level's strategies, then implement them.

5. Reassess progress frequently.

I hope that you're now feeling confident about the path forward, and that the book helps you to reduce the complexity of your improvement journey and to increase its chance of success.

I look forward to hearing your story. Write to me at gbroza@3PVantage.com.

Please write a brief review

Your insights and takeaways can make a significant impact in helping other professionals discover the value of this book. If you believe it can benefit them, please consider taking a few moments to share your thoughts by leaving a review or rating on the platform where you bought the book or on Goodreads. Your feedback, no matter how brief, goes a long way in spreading the knowledge and wisdom contained within these pages. Thank you!

GROUP DISCUSSION QUESTIONS FOR IMPROVEMENT LEADERS

Having focused conversations about the book's concepts with your fellow improvement leaders will amplify shared ownership and prepare you to apply its guidance. After you have all read the book and before you initiate any changes, kick off discussions using questions chosen from the following list. Pose them in the order they appear here, and work on them one at a time. Consider inviting every participant to spend a few minutes writing down their answers *in silence*, and then study the inputs together.

REFLECTION AND INTERPRETATION

1. How have you applied system thinking at work?

2. What important, surprising, or impactful things have you learned about using system thinking at work from reading *Deliver Better Results*?

3. In what ways has the organization been putting people first?

4. What new insights and perspectives do you have about the human side of work?

5. What was the most memorable or impactful story, example, or quote in the book? Why did it stand out to you?

6. What work phenomena, behaviors, and situations are you now seeing in a new light?

7. How does the book challenge or support your mindset, opinions, or assumptions about value delivery?

8. What was the most useful or valuable advice, technique, or caution that you took away from this book?

9. How will applying the book's guidance improve your system's ability to execute on the company's strategy?

APPLICATION

10. What are some examples of upcoming situations you might handle differently after reading the book?

11. Now that you know about the system side of value delivery, what fundamental changes might you like to make to how you lead and engage others? What sort of habits might you wish to adopt?

12. Recall past attempts to improve value delivery: some that succeeded and were sustainable, some that succeeded only in the short term, and some that didn't work. What contributed (perhaps indirectly) to the outcome in each case? Which of these insights would you factor into your improvement plans?

13. Which leadership behaviors and actions will be particularly effective in improving your system?

14. What strategies, techniques, or pieces of advice from this book do you think will be very difficult to apply, and why? What needs to change to make them easier to apply?

15. Thinking about the pathway to implementing the book's strategies (explained in Chapter 4), where do you see the biggest challenge? How can you overcome it?

16. On the journey of change, what will you do and avoid doing to foster healthy and enduring improvements?

17. The company has obligations and plans, and work never stops. How will you make the time and space to make change happen?

 SUPPLEMENTARY RESOURCE: Download "Group Discussion Questions" (the above questions in a Word document) from the book's companion website, DeliverBetterResultsBook.com.

If you'd like my assistance in facilitating and enriching these discussions, reach out to me at gbroza@3PVantage.com.

THE STORY OF A JOURNEY FROM LEVEL 1 TO 4 IN TEN MONTHS

This software company had about 50 people, most of whom worked in product development. In 2019, a leading corporation acquired this company, but kept it as a mostly independent division. In early 2021, new senior managers rolled out Scrum, and in December 2021, I conducted an assessment of product development. I found that fitness was at Level 1 (raw score of 8) and that Agile was an appropriate choice for their goals and context. (As a reminder, the raw fitness score maps to the fitness levels as follows. 6-8: Level 1; 9-11: Level 2; 12-13: Level 3; 14-16: Level 4; 17-18: Level 5.)

In January 2022, everyone took my Agile Fundamentals course, which is equal parts mindset and tactics. I then facilitated Strategy 1b (design the way of working), first with all the managers, then looping in the team leads as well. Management, in consultation with the staff, shifted some product roles, adjusted the Scrum teams' membership based on product needs and technical expertise, and upgraded the team lead role. They also canceled an inefficient weekly cross-team meeting, replacing it with offline updates.

The company had *many* initiatives in progress, each assigned to a separate person, including many contractors. As a result, teams weren't really teams. Calling management's attention to the consequences of this dynamic was enough to get action. The head of product captured *every* initiative in a roadmapping tool and then narrowed the list down. Later, he'd narrow it down even more.

By March, the system was at Level 2 (raw score 11) and the leads all felt positive about the progress and structure. The roadmap was now the single source of truth. They stabilized the system, specifically by reducing WIP and cleaning up backlogs, and streamlined status tracking. In collaborative workshops, folks wrote charters for each of the top 10 roadmap items, which increased clarity and alignment and facilitated the sequencing of the work involved in each. Top leadership was laying the groundwork for some role shifts to address inconsistencies in high-level decision-making. When I pointed out to them that teams were quietly skeptical that the changes were for real, the leadership committed to be more proactive and transparent, and to be explicit about the behaviors they expected from the teams.

The company was used to putting out a major release every six months, which is not unreasonable in their field. In April, they were finalizing the mid-year release and planning the next one. They didn't reduce the six-month cadence yet, but did change their approach to commitments and to intermediate releases: every two months there'd be a feature release (as opposed to just a bug-fix one), and it'd be a "train" release: any feature that wasn't ready would wait for the next release. The roadmap's ownership shifted from the founder to the product management team, and the roadmap started including sequenced outcomes with suggested, rather than binding, dates. Product Development collaborated weekly with Marketing to minimize surprises and maximize Marketing's lead time. Teams were reducing their WIP, which helped them finish more sprints as planned.

By mid-year, the system made it to Level 3. Team touchpoints were becoming more collaborative and worth having. The company took everyone to a three-day off-site for strategy discussions, team building, and all-voices-heard "What should we do next" discussions. There was a noticeable but still small increase in people's perceived safety and their collaboration, two matters we had tried unsuccessfully to improve at Level 2.

Conducting SQUARE's fitness assessment (see Chapter 1) in August, all aspects were "midway," except cost-efficiency, which was "near"; the system was at the top end of Level 3. Product reviewed the roadmap frequently, and had streamlined a process for regularly bringing requirements, feedback, and internal improvements into it. There were earnest discussions about reducing release lengths and moving to frequent deployments. Team members, who had previously sat silent in sprint planning meetings while the team leader and PO spoke, were now participating actively. There was more collaboration between developers and content team members. Lower-level strategies were becoming more habitual and more effective: leaders were constantly keeping a viable limit on roadmap items (which was hard for them!), breaking work down better, and ensuring decision-ownership clarity.

Despite all the progress, many issues remained. The top issues were dependencies between teams, frequent breakage due to code changes, scope management and planning, and consistency of messaging around release dates. Nevertheless, when the owning corporation ran their ecosystem-wide engagement survey in October, this division was the only one that came out all green. Every score was between 85% and 100%, with the highest-scoring aspects being belief in the mission, alignment, team, safety, equality, and autonomy.

The company was pursuing a major revamp of the product's UI in the second half of the year. Any other year, they'd have executed it as a Waterfall project. Instead, they demonstrated considerable agility, creating a task team that evolved the design and the implementation, testing and iterating continuously. Facing another significant initiative a few months later, they had an easier time adapting their team structure and processes.

The last I worked with them was November 2022, as their raw fitness score reached 15 (Level 4). My total involvement up to that point included only the initial assessment and mapping of the Agile journey, three course sessions, facilitating an Open Space at the off-site, and 30 half-days of coaching and consulting spread across the year. I attribute much of their success to management's consistent and aligned commitment to creating agility.

APPENDIX C

AGILE TRANSFORMATIONS/JOURNEYS AND THIS BOOK'S MODEL

Many organizations try to improve the fitness for purpose aspects presented in Chapter 1 — throughput, adaptability, outcomes, timeliness, consistency, and cost-efficiency. Some of those organizations consider the improvement a transformation, whereas others think of it as a journey (which implies that it's a gradual undertaking that takes time). It's an *Agile* transformation or journey if it aims to replace the current way of working with one based on Agile mindset and tactics. Where Agile is indeed a right fit, this should result in improvement to all six fitness aspects.

The devil, as usual, is in the details. *How* do you *effectively* navigate a change to Agile? My answer is: follow this book's model (SQUARE). If Agile is indeed a suitable approach for your system's needs — which is determined as part of implementing Strategy 1b — then the journey is to implement each fitness level's strategies based on Agile choices.

Of course, SQUARE is not the only model for creating real agility. However, the premises it rests on suggest three explanations for why some attempts fall short of their intended goals:

- They don't address the entire value delivery system. They pay some attention to adaptability and outcomes, but otherwise focus on the build part, aiming to increase development throughput and timeliness. This is often apparent in how those organizations interpret "high performing teams."

- They overwhelm the targeted parts of the system with many simultaneous changes. Leaders set up teams, roll out processes and practices, encourage collaboration, involve teams in planning, increase release frequency, and do much more — all at the same time. Even when the chosen changes are theoretically right for system fitness (which isn't always the case), and even with coaching support, the system absorbs only some of the changes, which creates conflicts and tensions.

- They (especially "transformations") are run with a flip-the-switch mentality. However, real agility tends to be very different from the current mindset, and people rarely change theirs in one fell swoop. Further complicating matters, big-bang Agile adoptions are often heavy on standardizing process and light on supporting people.

If your company has already started an Agile journey transformation, use this book's model to assess its current fitness, start necessary conversations, lay the necessary leadership foundation, and focus on the strategies that matter the most now.

FURTHER READING

If you've found this book useful, you might like my other writing as well. Every week (since 2009), I send out a free newsletter containing insights and solutions for common value delivery situations. As a subscriber, you'll also be the first to hear about my next projects and about subscriber-exclusive opportunities to learn from me.

You can sign up at 3PVantage.com/newsletter.

Saying that this book's subject is broad is an under-statement. Its insights and advice echo those written in many separate books. In each chapter, I had to limit the depth of the information I included in order to keep the book's length reasonable. To go deeper with a topic, look for my recommended book or online resource in the following list.

CHAPTER 1: THE BIG PICTURE

My book *The Agile Mind-Set* (3P Vantage Media, 2015) provides a pragmatic and method-agnostic exploration of what being Agile is like. For complete guidance on creating such a way of working in non-software contexts, read my later book *Agile for Non-Software Teams* (3P Vantage Media, 2019).

CHAPTER 2: UNDERSTANDING SYSTEMS OF VALUE DELIVERY

Thinking in Systems by Donella Meadows (Chelsea Green, 2008) provides a very accessible, nontechnical explanation of system thinking.

Esther Derby's post *Shaping Patterns* talks about leading effectively in a system by attending to clarity, conditions, and constraints (estherderby.com/shaping-patterns).

CHAPTER 3: LEADING FITNESS IMPROVEMENTS

The Speed of Trust by Stephen M.R. Covey (Simon & Schuster, 2006) provides a tangible structure for understanding interpersonal trust and behavioral advice for creating it.

In *Lead Without Blame* by Diana Larsen and Tricia Broderick (Berrett-Koehler, 2022) you'll find tools and perspectives for healthy leadership.

Taking responsibility when things go wrong (and inspiring it in others) is a hallmark of leadership. Christopher Avery's *The Responsibility Process* (Partnerwerks, 2016) explains the thinking patterns that help us take responsibility or hold us back from doing so. It's a game-changer for both personal and work life.

Atomic Habits by James Clear (Avery, 2018) provides an effective approach to building lasting habits while breaking bad ones.

On the matter of language, two impactful books are:

- L. David Marquet's *Leadership Is Language* (Portfolio, 2020) demonstrates how leaders can achieve better outcomes by choosing what they say and don't say.

- Shelle Rose Charvet's *Words That Change Minds* (Institute for Influence, 2019) describes little-known mental filters, called "metaprograms," that affect how people speak and listen and thereby impact their ability to influence others.

CHAPTER 4: EXECUTING THE IMPROVEMENT STRATEGIES

John P. Kotter's *Leading Change* (Harvard Business Review Press, 2012) is a still-relevant classic on creating meaningful change in organizations. Esther Derby's *7 Rules for Positive, Productive Change* (Berrett-Koehler, 2019) provides powerful advice for approaching change in a gradual and empowering way. For a more scientific take on managing change in complex adaptive systems, read *Facilitating Organization Change* by Edwin Olson and Glenda Eoyang (Pfeiffer, 2001).

As you lead changes to the way of working, folks may resist you, your mode of delivery, or your message. My first book, *The Human Side of Agile* (3P Vantage Media, 2012) has an entire chapter on defusing resistance.

The Story Factor by Annette Simmons (Basic Books, 2002) is an easy read, providing practical storytelling advice for inspiration, influence, and persuasion.

CHAPTER 5, STRATEGY 1A: MANAGE THE PROJECT PORTFOLIO

Melissa Perri's *Escaping the Build Trap* (O'Reilly Media, 2018) explains how to connect the portfolio's contents to the product strategy.

Johanna Rothman's *Manage Your Project Portfolio* (Pragmatic Bookshelf, 2009) provides detailed guidance on everything involved in creating and maintaining a usable portfolio.

In *Why I Invented the Now-Next-Later Roadmap*, Janna Bastow explains this simple and effective format for roadmaps (prodpad.com/blog/invented-now-next-later-roadmap).

CHAPTER 5, STRATEGY 1B: DESIGN THE WAY OF WORKING

If your way of working follows an Agile model:

- My book *The Agile Mindset* (3P Vantage Media, 2015) dives deep into values, beliefs, and principles and their manifestation in tactics, specifically in an Agile context.

- Jeff Anderson's *Organizing Toward Agility* (Agile By Design Publications, 2022) will help you design, grow, and sustain an appropriate structure.

- For advice on organizing for flow, see *Team Topologies* by Matthew Skelton and Manuel Pais (IT Revolution Press, 2019).

For more on the implications of Conway's Law (observation, really), read Martin Fowler's thoughtful post (martinfowler.com/bliki/ConwaysLaw.html, retrieved August 2, 2023).

Find useful insights and techniques for team self-selection in Sandy Mamoli and David Mole, *Creating Great Teams* (The Pragmatic Bookshelf, 2015).

Heidi Helfand's *Dynamic Reteaming* (O'Reilly, 2020) provides perspectives and techniques for changing team composition as the system evolves.

CHAPTER 6, STRATEGY 2A: SORT OUT DECISION-MAKING

A possible model for decision rights is the DACI matrix (project-management.com/daci-model/), which identifies the Driver, Approver, Contributor, and Informed for each key decision.

Delegation Poker (management30.com/practice/delegation-poker/), a practice from *Management 3.0*, helps groups articulate the level of delegation for each decision.

For techniques that groups can use to make decisions, see Michael Wilkinson, *The Secrets of Facilitation* (Jossey-Bass, 2012) and Jean Tabaka, *Collaboration Explained* (Addison-Wesley Professional, 2006).

CHAPTER 6, STRATEGY 2B: STABILIZE THE SYSTEM

The matter of system stability is based on the work of Dr. W. Edwards Deming, who taught Japanese (and later American) companies to appreciate and manage their systems. For a modern-day, thought-provoking take on his work, read Christopher Chapman's blog *The Digestible Deming*.

Read about variation and common vs. special causes in *Understanding Variation* by Henry Neave (demingalliance.

org/resources/articles/understanding-variation-the-springboard-for-process-improvement).

Making Work Visible by Dominica DeGrandis (IT Revolution Press, 2022) provides advice on, well, making work visible.

Limiting WIP and managing delays are two key concepts in the Kanban method. Many Kanban resources explain them in depth.

For research, insights, and resources regarding metrics, visit the website of Troy Magennis (focusedobjective.com). If your teams use an Agile way of working, Doc Norton's *Escape Velocity* (Onbelay Consulting, 2020) provides a deep dive into suitable metrics.

Learn about process behavior charts in Christopher Chapman, *Control Charts: Stop Chasing Down Causes (digestibledeming.substack.com/p/control-charts)*.

CHAPTER 7, STRATEGY 3A: INCREASE SAFETY, TEAMWORK, AND COLLABORATION

Timothy Clark's *The 4 Stages of Psychological Safety* (Berrett-Koehler, 2020) provides practical guidance on creating safety.

To gauge and possibly increase safety in a meeting, start it with a safety check: an anonymous poll of the participants' willingness to discuss potentially risky matters. For more detail, see this post (stevenmsmith.com/ar-safety-check/) from Steven Smith and this post (blog.gdinwiddie.com/2012/02/06/safety-exercise/) from George Dinwiddie.

On teamwork, a still-relevant classic is Patrick Lencioni's *The Five Dysfunctions of a Team* (Jossey-Bass, 2002). *Teams Unleashed* by Phillip Sandahl and Alexis Phillips (Nicholas Brealey, 2019) provides coaching tools for building team effectiveness.

My first book, *The Human Side of Agile* (3P Vantage Media, 2012), recommends that an Agile team include the role of a team leader, whose purpose is to support the team's evolution to greatness. The book provides extensive guidance on how to do that.

HBR's 10 Must Reads on Collaboration (Harvard Business Review, 2013) contains 10 of the best articles on working productively with colleagues.

CHAPTER 7, STRATEGY 3B: DEFER COMMITMENTS AND INCREASE RELEASE FREQUENCY

Accelerate by Nicole Forsgren, Jez Humble, and Gene Kim (IT Revolution Press, 2018) provides advice on system elements that make frequent releases possible.

Commitment by Olav Maassen, Chris Matts, and Chris Geary (Hathaway te Brake, 2016) teaches when to commit and when to leave options open. It does that in an uncommon way: it's a graphic novel.

CHAPTER 7, STRATEGY 3C: ENGAGE TEAMS IN PLANNING

Jean Tabaka's *Collaboration Explained* (Addison-Wesley Professional, 2006) teaches facilitation specifically for software leaders.

CHAPTER 8, STRATEGY 4A: EXPAND TEAM OWNERSHIP

For a powerful example of creating real ownership in an organization used to top-down control — a nuclear submarine — see L. David Marquet's *Turn the Ship Around!* (Portfolio, 2013).

Find useful insights and techniques for team self-selection in Sandy Mamoli and David Mole, *Creating Great Teams* (The Pragmatic Bookshelf, 2015).

A team is "ensembling" or "mobbing" when all the members are collaborating on one task instead of working on separate tasks. Learn about this approach in Woody Zuill's *Software Teaming* (2022). I've worked with teams that used it also for non-software tasks.

CHAPTER 8, STRATEGY 4B: IMPROVE DECISION-MAKING

In the context of product management choices, Itamar Gilad's Confidence Meter (itamargilad.com/the-tool-that-will-help-you-choose-better-product-ideas/) is a handy tool for assessing confidence.

Rich Mironov's article *Product Waste and The ROI of Discovery* makes a good case for improving discovery as a way to reduce the negative outcomes of product waste (mironov.com/waste).

Ron Kohavi's book *Trustworthy Online Controlled Experiments* (Cambridge University Press, 2020) provides real world guidance for data-driven decision-making. Also listen to his podcast interview with Lenny Rachitsky (lennyspodcast.com/the-ultimate-guide-to-ab-testing-ronny-kohavi-airbnb-microsoft-amazon/), which is packed with impactful insights about experimentation.

The article *Strong Opinions, Weakly Held* by Ameet Ranadive explains this method well (medium.com/@ameet/strong-opinions-weakly-held-a-framework-for-thinking-6530d417e364).

Find great insights on interleaving discovery and delivery in *Continuous Discovery Habits* by Teresa Torres (Product Talk, 2021).

CHAPTER 8, STRATEGY 4C: REDUCE THE TECHNICAL COST OF CHANGE

Michael Feathers' classic *Working Effectively with Legacy Code* (Pearson, 2004) remains relevant for many present-day software systems. Another classic is *Growing Object-Oriented Software, Guided by Tests* by Steve Freeman and Nat Pryce (Addison-Wesley Professional, 2009).

For more on working with technical agility, see Chapter 7 in my book *The Agile Mind-Set* (3P Vantage Media, 2015).

ACKNOWLEDGMENTS

You might think that after writing three books, writing the fourth is easy. Nope. The fitness for purpose of my book writing system (*see what I did there?*) may be high, but the work is still difficult. Fortunately, I was not alone.

I'm blessed to know many kind and knowledgeable people, whose feedback helped make this book what it is: Jay Allison, Pete Anderson, Dave Barrett, Kerstin Bresler, Debbie Brey, Tricia Broderick, Chris Chapman, Andrei Cornienco, Dinah Davis, David Frink, John Hill, Kenn Hussey, Gino Marckx, Johanna Rothman, Alon Sabi, Dan Snyder, Yael Soffer, Ilana Sprongl, Seetha Val, and DiDi Vaz. I'm also grateful to Jason Brucker, Tom Diedrich, Padmashree Koneti, Kamal Manglani, Chris Mause, Doc Norton, and Dann Wilson for their observations and encouragement. My thanks also go to all the leaders who contributed stories to the book, some of whom did not wish to fully identify themselves.

Many of the ideas, insights, and suggestions you've read came into being much earlier than the book: I put them forth in my weekly newsletter and LinkedIn posts. That content *never* goes out without getting a critical review from Ronit Andorn-Broza — my life partner, business partner, and collaborator-in-everything. And after it goes out, I get feedback from some of my thousands of subscribers and followers. Thank you all.

And where does all of it *really* begin? With my clients. The way I structure engagements enables me to personally support multiple clients every year and to stay involved long enough to see the effects of changes (and to learn a lot more in the process). Having this view into the workings of dozens of companies, which develop all sorts of products and solutions, has shaped this book's model and provided almost all of its stories and examples. Dear clients, thank you for trusting me to help you deliver better results.

Gil Broza, Toronto, 2023

REFERENCES

CHAPTER 2

1. Russell Ackoff, *From Mechanistic to Systemic Thinking,* (youtube.com/watch?v=yGN5DBpW93g), a presentation at the System Thinking in Action conference, 1993.

2. Chip and Dan Heath, *Decisive: How to Make Better Choices in Life and Work* (Currency, 2013).

CHAPTER 3

1. Seth Godin, *Free Prize Inside* (Portfolio, 2007)

2. According to this post (deming.org/a-bad-system-will-beat-a-good-person-every-time/) by the Deming Institute, Dr. Deming made this statement in one of his seminars. (Retrieved August 2, 2023).

3. Daniel Pink, *Drive: The Surprising Truth About What Motivates Us* (Riverhead Trade, 2011). The book presents autonomy, mastery, and purpose as necessary conditions for motivation; in my unresearched opinion, enjoyability and challenge also belong in this list.

4. This description and drawing of the Satir model is based on Virginia Satir et al., *The Satir Model: Family Therapy and Beyond* (Science and Behavior Books, 1991), Gerald M. Weinberg, *Quality Software Management: Anticipating Change, vol. 4* (Dorset House, 1997), Steven Smith, *The Satir Change Model* (stevenmsmith.com/ar-satir-change-model/), and my own observations.

5. Timothy Clark, *The 4 Stages of Psychological Safety: Defining the Path to Inclusion and Innovation* (Berrett-Koehler, 2020).

6. Stephen M.R. Covey, *The Speed of Trust: The One Thing that Changes Everything* (Simon & Schuster, 2006).

CHAPTER 4

1. This might sound simplistic, but it's life-changing. I learned it from executive coach and close friend David Spann.

CHAPTER 6

1. RACI matrix (project-management.com/understanding-responsibility-assignment-matrix-raci-matrix/)

2. Several business books teach the Theory of Constraints, including Eliyahu Goldratt's classic novel *The Goal*, first published in the 80's and focused on manufacturing, and Clarke Ching's *Rolling Rocks Downhill* (2014) which focuses on agile software development.

3. Johanna Rothman, *Why Minimize Management Decision Time* (jrothman.com/mpd/management/2020/08/why-minimize-management-decision-time/).

4. Nicole Forsgren, Jez Humble, and Gene Kim, Accelerate: *The Science of Lean Software and DevOps: Building and Scaling High Performing Technology Organizations* (IT Revolution Press, 2018).

CHAPTER 7

1. Pavel Samsonov, *Design is the art of being wrong safely.* (spavel.medium.com/design-is-the-art-of-being-wrong-safely-7575b0c395c2).

2. Beyond Budgeting (bbrt.org).

INDEX

MEET GIL BROZA

Value Delivery & Leadership Expert and Owner, 3P Vantage, Inc.
Email contact: gbroza@3PVantage.com

Gil Broza specializes in helping tech leaders deliver far better results by upgrading their Agile ways of working. He also supports their non-software colleagues in creating real business agility in their teams. He has helped over 100 large and small, private- and public-sector  organizations achieve real, sustainable improvements by working with their unique contexts and focusing on mindset, culture, and leadership. Previously, Gil worked as a development manager, team leader, and programmer for many years, successfully applying Agile methods since 2001. He has served as a regular writer for the prestigious magazine *projectmanagement.com* (a PMI publication) and as a track chair for the Agile 2009, 2010, and 2016 conferences. He regularly gives keynotes and interactive talks at conferences worldwide.

Throughout his career, Gil has focused on human characteristics that prevent positive outcomes in teams and organizations. These include limiting habits, fear of change, outdated beliefs, and blind spots, among many others. In helping teams and leaders overcome these factors, he supports them in reaching ever-higher levels of performance, confidence, and accomplishment. In 2012, he published *The Human Side of Agile*, the definitive guide to leading Agile teams. In 2015, he published *The Agile Mind-Set*, helping practitioners and leaders alike master the Agile approach and make their ways of working truly effective. And in 2019, he published *Agile for Non-Software Teams* to help managers consider, design, start, and cultivate Agile ways of working in non-software functions.

Gil provides services for establishing effective ways of working and improving value delivery. Companies also invite Gil for specialized support, such as facilitating organizational mindset workshops, delivering keynote at internal conferences, and leading sessions with executives. See his current offerings at 3PVantage.com/services.

Printed in Great Britain
by Amazon

37085770R10145